TETHERED

A Healer's Ultimate Test

A story of healing, miracles, and love

By Peg Rodrigues

I dedicate this book to my four children—Logan, Madison, Makenzie, and Landon. You have all expanded my heart in different ways and shown me that love has the power to heal. Every single one of you has healed a piece of me and continues to teach me so much about myself.

And there would be no story if it weren't for my husband, Jim. I am so grateful that we get to complete this incarnation together.

Introduction

I always find the universe amusing. One minute, everything in your life seems orderly and neat, and the next, a simple health crisis can lead to a near-death experience and change your entire trajectory and the way you look at the world.

If there's one thing I've learned, it's that when crisis strikes, the lives of those impacted—especially loved ones—can be irreversibly transformed. But such crises can be the catalyst for the most massive healing you will ever experience, as long as you are ready for the journey ahead.

Tethered is my story of how I helped my husband recover and heal when he "died" three times after a pulmonary embolism and multiple cardiac arrests. For those who are struggling with formidable and seemingly insurmountable health issues, I hope my story offers a new way of framing your experience. I know without a doubt that the healing power of love makes it possible to come out on the other side with a deeper sense of meaning. As an energy healer, I also know what it truly means to surrender your agenda and allow the Divine to work through you.

The book is not meant to be an idealistic depiction of healing. I wrote the majority of it over a short period of time, as a raw, human, unembellished account of what it means to reconcile the mysteries of life and death with your lived experiences. This is a full account of all my own insecurities and doubts, and guidance of how to pull out of fear and come back to love. Through the process of living those terrifying 12 days and writing about my journey, I received a glimpse into what it means to return to our fundamental nature (love), in the midst of fear and panic. Unbeknownst to many people, even energy healers are not immune to the anxiety and despair that a health crisis can bring on!

In many ways, writing this book was my way of wrestling with life's major questions: Why are we here? What is our destiny? How do we surrender to the unpredictable nature of life? How do we find fruitful meaning and purpose in the midst of tragedy?

Everything that happened to my husband has continued to reverberate in the lives of our family, including our four children and extended family members. While we've had an enormous amount of support navigating our healing journey, with all its uncertainty and unanswered questions, I know that too many people go through similar experiences and are less fortunate.

In writing my story, I also feel that it's imperative to move beyond physical health to consider how we can care for our emotional and spiritual health, especially during the dark nights of the soul that accompany crisis.

With love and understanding, as well as the support of community, we can open ourselves up to genuine miracles. We can touch the unseen realms of energy, healing, and intuition in such a way that it will pave the path for the unthinkable to occur.

In many ways, this book is an account of my own real-life miracle. Jim wouldn't be alive today, and my family wouldn't remain intact, without the well-timed actions of several Earth angels. The kind words, prayers, and love that were transmitted to my family contributed to our healing. I had heard many times that the collective matters, but now I believe that to my core. And without a doubt love mobilizes transformation.

(Please note: Some names and details have been changed to protect the privacy of individuals.)

Contents

One: Shock and Awe

Once I figure out what that beeping noise is near my head, I pop awake and shut off my alarm. I have two modes, going like a bat out of hell, and dead asleep. I shake the sleep from my brain and switch into autopilot. As a mom of four children all going in different directions, I am deep in the chaos of life. To maintain even the smallest grip on reality, I have established as many routines to our days as I can muster. I shower quickly and walk downstairs to make sure everyone has breakfast and a packed lunch for the day.

My husband, Jim and I married when I was a young twenty-three year old, and quickly fell into an agreement that I would stay home and raise our four children, even though after the birth of our first child, I was in my mind, highly unqualified for such a task.

In a desperate attempt on my part to understand the mess I had made of my life by age thirty-five I signed up for a four-year earth energy healing school at the suggestion of a girlfriend. She saw I was drowning in motherhood and threw me a life preserver. Jim was working hard to keep a roof over our heads, feed our gaggle of children, and absolutely loved and adored me. By outside markers, I had a wonderful life, except for one problem, I felt completely disconnected from myself. No one had ever taught me to take care of myself, let alone know I had needs too. I think this is a common side effect of being a mom- we come last.

I had no idea the quest to save myself would lead to one day playing a pivotal role in saving my husband. There are some things you just assume (foolishly, I might add) like you are going to wake up every morning and still be able to talk, walk and breathe. So, on a random Wednesday morning in November 2016 this was the falsehood I clung to when I started my day.

I credit the healing school for not only saving me but giving me a purpose and a passion. Everything in my life has improved, I have started my own healing practice, and I learned how to take care of myself first, digging deep within and becoming courageous, learning how to have the hard conversations, and now I live a life filled with integrity and truth. My outsides and insides finally match up.

The school also taught me to be intuitive and trust those feelings. Right now, Spirit (my name for my intuitive voice), has an urgent message it keeps thrusting into my mind as I am simultaneously scrambling to get three of our children into the car at 6:45 a.m. to drive them to school.

"Jim's coloring is off."

Little did I know this message Spirit is whispering to me will become a defining moment that will alter the course of our lives forever. Life has markers, a line in the sand. There will forever be our life before November 2, 2016 and our life after. If only I knew our family is hanging on the edge of one of these moments.

"Are you sure you're OK?" I ask Jim, pausing a moment after grabbing my keys.

"If I get worse, I'll drive myself to urgent care," he reassures me. "Don't worry, I'll be fine."

That should be my clue that everything isn't "fine." He had used that word to describe how he felt after ripping his foot open and getting hit by a car. "I'm fine," he'd insisted.

Jim hasn't been feeling well for a few days. He had a weird cough in the middle of the night Sunday, and then he was super tired on Monday, even falling asleep in the car while our daughter had a workout session with her personal trainer. On Tuesday he sat on the couch all day and watched movies, complaining he was worn out.

Maybe a virus? When he came up to bed last night, his breathing was hard and labored. I insisted that we go to the ER, but true to form, he refused.

Jim was born and raised in the town of Fairhaven, Massachusetts, which is located an hour south of Boston. Over 22 years of marriage, I've learned that his East Coast attitude of strength and perseverance has served him well— and at other times, it gets in his way. Add to that his Portuguese heritage: proud, stubborn, and at times unyielding. In other words, I've figured out when to pick my battles.

Now it's Wednesday morning, and I'm starting to get concerned. Jim is my rock. He is never sick, and he rarely complains about anything. But by now, I should be aware that when he goes down, he goes down big. Fourteen years ago, he blew a disc in his neck and went into paralysis before they did emergency surgery. Eleven years ago, he ripped his foot open on a lava rock in Hawaii, which should've received immediate medical attention and stitches, but instead, he cleaned the wound and wrapped it up. Five years ago, he was crushed between two cars in India, and instead of going to a hospital, he flew home to Seattle.

At this point, I should be attuned to the fact that we just might be due for another one of Jim's big health events.

But I simply shrug and say, "I love you," bundle the kids up, and off we go.

My morning carpool starts when I drop my oldest daughter, Madison, off at the local high school. Next up, I drive my second daughter, Makenzie, to her school about a half hour away. By the time I arrive, Spirit is speaking louder, poking at me, asking me to pay attention to it.

"Jim's coloring is off."

Ding, ding, ding!

I decide to call his mother, who's a nurse. First, I try her home phone: no answer. Next, I try her cell. Hmmm, still nothing.

Next up in the mommy carpool, I drop off my younger son, Landon, at his school. By the time I get there at 7:45 a.m., I am deep in rumination about Jim's heavy breathing as he was walking up the stairs the night before. And now, his coloring is off!

My intuition is starting to ding even louder.

As an energy healer who sees four clients a day, I push aside my intuitive hits and shift my thoughts to the lunch I'll need a few hours from now. I head to Whole

Foods, where I opt for salmon and rice. Spirit is getting more insistent: *"SOMETHING IS WRONG WITH YOUR HUSBAND."*

One of the concepts I learned in my four year healing school was that when the universe is trying to talk to you, at first you get pebbles thrown your way, small nudges (Jim's coloring is off), then rocks (something is wrong with your husband), and if you're really not listening, the universe throws boulders.

You guessed it: here comes the boulder- in a deep booming voice I hear *"TURN AROUND."* I glance around my car, expecting to see a man in my backseat, instead I realize that "Spirit" is now shouting at me.

I pull over and shakily text my 9 a.m. client: "My husband is ill, and I need to take him to urgent care, so I have to cancel. Can we reschedule?" Worried now, and having learned to listen to my intuition, I turn my car around and head home.

Just as I'm pulling into the driveway, Jim texts an update that he's OK. Well, too bad, I'm already home. I go upstairs, and demand that he get dressed so I can take him to the ER.

He's still in bed and doesn't even protest. "Yeah, I'm definitely feeling off," he says. But first, before we head out, he needs to cancel everything that's on his plate for the day. Jim transferred to Seattle 24 years ago to work at Microsoft. It was a big deal to leave his close-knit family, but his drive and work ethic led him to seek out a high-powered job.

I start a crockpot of stew meat chili, clean the kitchen, and wait for Jim to come downstairs. When he finally shows up, he's heaving like a freight train. He tries to drink a little orange juice and then asks me to get some of his clothes and his knee brace, courtesy of a recent surgery to repair his left ACL. I quickly get him everything he asks for and help him dress at the kitchen table.

"Can you pull the car around to the front door, honey? I don't think I can make it to the garage," he wheezes.

Shit, this isn't good.

After I've brought the car out of the garage, I leave the front door open and come back to walk him out. Jim makes it about halfway before he stops at the stairs. "Can you give me a moment to rest?" he asks.

He sits down on the third step. In seconds, my husband goes into a full seizure.

I barely have time to react as Jim's eyes roll into the back of his head. His airway sounds constricted, and his limbs are convulsing. I grab him and hold him tight to prevent him from hitting his head on the step.

"Call 911!" I scream upstairs to Logan, our nineteen year old son, who's still asleep after working late the night before.

My poor kid quickly comes sliding down the hall like Kramer on *Seinfeld*, wide-eyed and with terror in his voice. "What's happening, Mom?"

Jim suddenly sits up. His pupils are dilated. He looks at me, obviously disoriented. "Sorry, sorry, I'm OK, sorry," he mumbles.

Then, his eyes widen and he mouths a question to me: "Clot?"

WHAT THE HELL IS GOING ON? Is he throwing a blood clot?

At this point, Logan is on the phone with the 911 operator. Unsurprisingly, he is shaken up and doesn't know the answers to the questions she is asking him.

"Give me the phone!" I yell. I do my best to answer the operator's questions: "What is Jim's date of birth? Was he healthy prior to this moment? Is he a smoker or drinker? What do you think is going on?"

"How much longer until they get here?" I ask, the hysteria rising in my voice. At the same time, I am holding

Jim upright in my arms, asking him to keep breathing and stay with me. I only have one thought: *I want my kids to have a father.*

I am not even concerned about me. I have lived a beautiful life with this man as my husband. I'm more worried about my 11-year-old son, in particular. There is something about the father-son bond that is so vital, especially at Landon's age—and I know I simply can't fill Jim's shoes.

My mind is racing with all these crazy thoughts as I'm waiting for the ambulance:

My kids need a father.

I haven't done CPR in 20 years, so please get here quick.

My husband can't die—he's only 51 years old.

Oh my God, is that what is happening here??? Is he dying???

I pull my mind back to the present. "Logan, move the car out of the driveway!" I bark, realizing by the tone in my voice I am starting to panic. He gets on it immediately. In the meantime, Jim's breathing gets more and more labored as the minutes tick by. His coloring, which I was so worried about this morning, is now light blue. He's giving me the same look my daughter Madison did when she was three years old and started to drown in the pool. Unable to speak, eyes pleading for help. Something I will never forget.

Thank God the EMTs show up right then.

One of them directs me to let go of Jim; they've got him now. They immediately get oxygen on him and search for a pulse. Observing the EMTs as they shoot worried looks back and forth, I realize how much trouble Jim is in. That's when I feel myself truly beginning to panic. They radio for more help. I try to reassure myself: Soon, our hallway will be full of emergency personnel.

Three paramedics, who arrived quickly after the EMTs called for backup, lay Jim on the floor and I move to his head.

Jim points and says, "I feel something in my throat." They remove the oxygen mask from his face, he turns his head to the left and hocks up a loogie on the rug.

Then he looks straight into my eyes and says, "I love you."

As I take a breath, letting his words sink into my soul, Jim exhales his last, and dies right in our front hallway.

Life has dropped a marker. From this point forward there will be life prior to this moment, and our life after. I will forever use "well, Jim's not dead on the floor" as my gauge for good days versus bad.

**

Jim has had his first cardiac arrest, at which point everyone goes into high gear, there is a life to be saved. I am quickly swished out of the way to make space for the growing number of paramedics, EMTs, and firefighters trying to save my husband. Logan is swirling in circles like a Tasmanian Devil, muttering "What the fuck is happening?" over and over. It is a question to which I have no answers. I can't even comfort my son right now. I feel like I'm underwater, or in a bad dream.

Tell me this isn't happening.

All I know is that it's "clinical death." Jim has no pulse. His heart has stopped, and he is no longer breathing. They cut his shirt off so quickly I don't see them do it. A paramedic jams something called an intraosseous infusion (IO) into my husband's right shin bone. This gives his body necessary fluids and medication when intravenous access isn't feasible. When you die, they have to move quickly to get you back. All I can think of as I watch the flurry of activity is that it looks like they're sticking my husband with something you jam into a tree to get maple syrup out of it.

Oh my God, they are screwing it into his
leg...maybe they are trying to get maple syrup out of my
husband.

I learn later that it's the easiest way to get epinephrine into his body to start up his heart again. I also learn that the reason the paramedic had to screw it into Jim's leg is that the battery on the IO machine died. (Seriously?!)

I've now entered what I call the "trauma swirl." Certain memories are crystal clear, others are fuzzy, our mind taking over to lessen the impact. After the IO needle being jammed into Jim's leg, the next clear picture is a female paramedic named Lafond lying on the floor head to head with my husband. He's on his back, and she's on her stomach, trying to intubate Jim. "I need a pillow!" she screams out, as Jim begins to bite down.

Lafond succeeds in getting him intubated, then the swarm of paramedics and firefighters roll a gurney down the driveway into the house, load Jim up to transport him to the hospital, and just like that, he's gone. All three of the paramedics are in the aid car, still working to save him.

A battalion chief, Tom, and a captain are left in my house. Whenever you have a "CPR event," higher officials in the emergency response command are called in to "manage the scene." (Code words for how crazy the people left behind are.) I glance at Tom and say, "It looks like a crime scene." He quickly assures me that they'll clean up. But I don't even care about that. I just need to speak in order to make sure this is all really happening.

"Where is he going?" I ask.

"Evergreen. It's the closest hospital."

For some reason, Tom's words terrify me.

Oh, they don't think he's going to make it.

The situation is dire. My husband of 22 years just died on our floor.

Tom looks at me, obviously concerned. "Do you want a ride to the hospital?

I shake my head emphatically. No. If my husband dies in the hospital, I want to be able to drive away quickly and never look back. I definitely need an out.

Tom looks at me calmly. He's been through this before more than once, no doubt. "Who do you need to call?"

The dreaded question. I don't want to call anyone and tell them this news. But I force myself to call Jim's mom first. Again, no answer. Then I call his brother.

At this point, the only thing we know for sure is that Jim was in full cardiac arrest. I am hysterical, but Jim's brother Dave tries to calm me. "Do I need to get my parents on a plane, Peg?"

"YES, please!" Jim's entire family lives in Boston, a five plus hour flight to Seattle.

I hang up and turn to Logan. "I need you to get your siblings from school, because I will be at the hospital with Dad." I feel guilty leaving my oldest son in a house where his dad just died on the floor by himself, but I don't have any other options.

There is no time to consider the implications of what's happening. But together, we have just witnessed something that no one should ever see. I know in that tender moment of connection that my older son and I will never be the same.

**

I try to keep it together as I jump in the car and drive to Evergreen Hospital, about 15 minutes away. I run through the list of people to call in my head: At the top of the list are my parents (who don't answer when I call them) and my sister (who's in Mexico on her first real family vacation, so no answer there, either).

I try my mom's cell phone twice more, then call my brother, Mike, who miraculously answers. I learn later that he had been in the woods hunting near his house in Clancy,

Montana, and simply had a gut feeling that he needed to go home. As soon as he got into cell phone range I called. As we begin talking, I realize I need him more than I knew. He's an EMT, and I will require his knowledge to guide me through my new reality.

Mike can't understand much of what I'm saying in my hysteria, but I am grateful that he doesn't question me or hesitate. He immediately books a flight.

Where the hell is everyone on a random Wednesday morning in November?

Clearly, most of my friends are busy. That's when I remember my sweet Aunt Peggy, whom I am named after. She lives in Kirkland, which is not too far from Evergreen. I call and ask her to meet me at the ER. Her "yes, I'll be right there" is an immediate relief. I need someone by my side to help me through this.

The rest of the drive is a blur, and I am grateful that I'm familiar with Evergreen, where three of my babies were delivered. The parking fairies don't let me down— there is one spot open right in front of the ER. I pull in too fast, and rush inside. "I'm here to see my husband, Jim Rodrigues," I tell the nurse at the desk. I can see the momentary cloud come over her face, and my stomach falls.

Please tell me Jim is still alive.

A charge nurse leads me into the ER. When she realizes that Jim is still being worked on, I am quickly ushered into a back-corner room. I can see the flurry of commotion around him, and my heart sinks. They won't let me see Jim until they get him stable, but for now, I can sense they are still trying to save him.

The nurse asks me if I want a chaplain to read Jim his last rites. Without thinking, I quickly respond, "No!" My husband is *NOT* dying today, so why on Earth would I need a priest?

Aunt Peggy shows up shortly afterwards. Again, a welcome wave of calm. Something about her demeanor helps soothe my crazy, overactive brain. She has a notebook with her. "I'll take notes, and we'll handle whatever comes up. Deal?" she says. I wonder what the hell taking notes is going to do, but I can feel that this simple mundane task is her way of trying to make sense of the situation. Because clearly, what is currently happening to my previously healthy, 51-year-old husband does not make any sense.

After waiting a short while, Dr. Harwich, the head ER doc, and Dr. Young, a pulmonologist, come in to brief us. "Jim is critical," Dr. Harwich says. "He kept going into cardiac arrest and coded multiple times this morning."

"We believe a DVT developed in Jim's left leg after his knee surgery on October 4th," Dr. Young gently explains. A DVT is a deep vein thrombosis, or a blood clot that forms deep in the veins and can be life-threatening. "This is causing blood clots to let loose and travel up to his lungs. His lungs are filled with clots, so when his heart tries to pump, it's clogged. This is called a pulmonary embolism."

I try to take in everything I'm being told. Dr Harwich explains, "Jim coded in your house, then again in the ambulance, then once more as he was being rolled into the ER. My staff and I took over CPR and made the decision with Dr. Young to administer an anticoagulant called tPA [Thrombolysis dosing for Activase, also known as alteplase].

Dr. Young continues, "We are going to continue to stabilize Jim and observe him. Head up to the CCU waiting room and we'll come find you when we get him upstairs."

As soon as they leave, Aunt Peggy and I exchange looks. Her lip is quivering but she stays calm. Neither of us wants to speak—it would make everything we were just told real. The charge nurse returns to show us to the CCU waiting room one floor up.

Jim and I will learn later, after meeting the paramedics, that he was one of the worst cases they had seen. They couldn't stabilize him, because with so many clots, his heart just kept shutting down. Imagine trying to pump something through sludge. But paramedics in the Seattle area are trained to never stop administering CPR. They call it high-impact CPR, which is made up of continuous chest compressions. The paramedic who was administering CPR on Jim simply traded with someone else every two minutes.

After meeting with the doctors and sinking into a chair in the CCU waiting room, I text Logan that his dad is "stabilized, running tests."

I am grateful for the information and the doctors' expertise, but it feels like I've walked into the Twilight Zone, or a very strange case study.

So much has happened in the last hour and a half. I have aged, that's for certain. Everything hurts: my heart, my head, my body. I look at Aunt Peggy and ask, "Can you go to my house to be with Logan and help him pick up Madison, Makenzie and Landon from school? And decide between the two of you who is going to break the news about their dad's collapse? Once you get them, I want them to come up to the CCU." She nods and gives me a wordless hug before heading out.

I sit down for a moment and gather myself. My first thought is to cancel the rest of my clients for the week. At this point, my friend Kelly shows up in the CCU. Ironic that she and I became close ten years ago, when we were in the middle of a crisis: losing a girlfriend to liver cancer. Kelly is stunned at this new turn of events. Anyone would be. This kind of thing happens to other people all the time. But Jim had been perfectly healthy, hardly ever went to the doctor, and had no issues with his heart. It's hard to believe that what's happening might be the result of a simple knee surgery.

Dr. Young walks into the CCU waiting room to discuss Jim's current state. "We're definitely pleased that Jim is alive," he says, although it's obvious that "shocked" is the word he wants to use. "We're still not in the clear yet, though. The next 24 hours are critical, and our biggest concern is internal bleeding."

Confused, I ask, "But didn't you administer the tPA to clear the blood clots?"

He nods. "Yes, but how that essentially works is that everything starts bleeding." He goes down a dizzyingly long list of possible side effects: bruising, bleeding, brain bleed, or a bleed in Jim's gastrointestinal tract, which would be the worst. He would just bleed out, and there would be nothing they could do.

I can't even think about that prospect. Luckily, Dr. Young isn't in discussion mode. He hurries back to be with Jim. Kelly is speechless. She gives me a big hug as I squeak out between tears, "I am *not* raising these kids on my own." Not after everything we've been through. Not after spending half my life with this man.

If that's all I get, I know I will ultimately be OK. But my kids would be cheated of all those little moments that matter. My girls wouldn't have a dad to walk them down the aisle, he wouldn't see his sons get married, he would never meet his grandchildren...and what would I do with all his comic books and the wine he loves to collect? I don't know the passwords to all his accounts. And, oh my God, our youngest son is only 11! Would life really be so cruel as to take his father *now*?

I call Jim's brother to give him an update and then text my own brother, who will come straight to the hospital when he lands. Then I call my other girlfriends: Wendy, a lifelong soul sister of 30 years; Maureen, my neighbor, who is like a second mom to my youngest son, Landon; and

Stephani, another friend who lives across the street from us. I cancel all the kids' appointments and my clients for the rest of the week, giving the short version of "my husband had a heart attack."

I know it's an awful bomb to drop in a conversation. But what else am I supposed to say? I'm not seeking empathy; at this point, everything feels very methodical and logistical. Wendy's husband works with Jim, so he is able to call Jim's boss and explain the situation, which I'm glad is off my list. I know I need to make as few calls as possible, with the greatest amount of results.

Two: Love Conquers All

Around noon, I am finally allowed to see Jim.

Oh. My. God.

No one could ever be prepared to see a loved one in such a state. All I can do is let the tears flow. Jim is unresponsive, on a ventilator, and cold to the touch. His hands are tied down, so he can't pull the ventilator out.

On the one hand, I am so grateful Jim is alive, but seeing him like this, I can't help but feel a new sense of dread wash over me. The ventilator tube has blood in it, something I try to see as a gentle reminder of the fight my husband has engaged in for his life. As I stand there assessing the whole situation, the knee surgeon calls and they patch him through into Jim's room. The surgeon sounds stunned by this turn of events.

Jim, like every other patient, was given a list of side effects, and had followed the surgery orders to the letter. He did pre-op and post-op physical therapy, and took baby aspirin to ward off the formation of DVTs. I guess it wasn't enough in Jim's case. I hang up and return to my husband's side.

When I touch him, I'm shocked by the coldness of his skin. One of the CCU nurses, Tonya, comes over and hands me Jim's wedding ring. She smiles at me, comfortingly. "I know that patients swell up from all the fluids and medicines that they pump into you, and we don't want him to lose a finger on top of everything else."

I momentarily flash back to the day we were married and I put that ring on his finger.

Funny to think of *till death do us part*.

I put it on my thumb until Jim can wear it again, and I smile at Tonya. "Thank you."

This simple act on the nurse's part becomes one in a list of little things that I can be grateful for, in the midst of this nightmare.

Being from Boston, Jim has a deep love for Patriots football. We recently watched a documentary about Bill Belichick, the head coach, who has a single requirement of his players: "DO YOUR JOB." Jim would be so proud. The reason he is still here at this moment is because everyone has done just that.

I hold Jim's hand.

Please, dear God, let him make it to the morning.

I can't explain why, but I feel that if he has gone through all these cardiac arrests and CPR, and is still with us at this moment, it means he has chosen to live.

Part of my training as an energy healer is to surrender to the "what is." Oh, have I surrendered. It feels like I'm at the beginning of a test I hadn't prepared for. I'm winging it, but I'm also relying on my gut instincts. I know from my training that you can set the stage for someone to heal themselves, but you can have no agenda with respect to what that looks like or how it manifests. Jim's healing is going to happen the way it needs to.

This inner strength I have learned to tune into gives me great comfort.

I am here to DO MY JOB.

"Peg, your only role is to hold space for Jim's healing, and to love him through it," I whisper to myself.

After all, love is the highest energetic vibration, because it has the power to heal.

Love will get me through this, love will get me through this…

That is all I can hold in my body, heart, and mind as I move through each hour of what is now becoming the longest day of my life.

I am still repeating this mantra to myself when, shortly after 4 p.m., all of my children arrive at the CCU waiting room with Logan and Aunt Peggy. I can see that they are all trying to put on their brave faces, but the fear in their eyes betrays them. I try to hug all of them at once. "It's going to be OK—your dad is alive," I whisper.

Because Jim's room in the CCU is small, I take two kids in at a time. The girls go first. I know my response was a big "holy shit" when I saw my husband in this state, so I can only imagine what the kids will think.

Makenzie starts to cry. "That is *not* Dad." Madison seconds her sister's sentiments with a shocked nod.

"Girls, go ahead and hold his hand and talk to him," I say softly. "It might not seem like he can hear you, but I think he does."

Madison is clearly not ready for any of this. "This feels like it's out of a movie," she says, shaking her head.

Tears are still pouring down Makenzie's face. "Mom, I thought he just had a cough."

The kids left for school thinking their dad had the flu, and now, nine hours later, he is clinging to life.

As a mom, I've been wrestling with this decision all day: Do I let my children see this? Will it be too traumatic? But the flip side is...*this is life*. Sometimes people get sick. Sometimes people die. But when I think of my girls' and boys' faces as they see their father hooked up to tubes and not responding, it's like my heart has been ripped out of my body. I want to take all that pain and swallow it for them, but I know that I need my strength.

Landon, our youngest, is the most painful reaction to witness. He is so innocent and hasn't yet encountered the ugly of the world. As I'm writing this, I can still hear Landon's sob as it leaves his throat. Still, I don't regret the decision to have them see their dad. After all, even though I don't want to think about it, it is still a very real possibility that he could die. We are only 6 hours into the 24-hour window of Jim potentially bleeding to death.

After they see their father, I hug and love on my kids to settle them down. I explain in simple terms what has happened and that I need to be here. Uncle Mike is flying in soon and will be their surrogate mom for tonight and the morning school run.

"You have each other to lean on," I assure them. "What will help me most of all is if you keep up a sense of normal."

I look at my daughters. "Especially for you girls. You're in high school and can't afford to fall behind in your classes. It will only hurt you in the long run. Ask for help from your teachers and school counselors. I'll email them and explain what happened to Dad."

"We'll do our best," Makenzie replies for both of them. Madison just nods. I know they're in shock and imagine it will be hard for them to concentrate at school, but I also know it's better for them to focus as much as they can on something other than what's happening right now.

After a round of hugs and kisses, the kids leave to find dinner and continue with their normal routines. Sometimes, as a mom, I feel like I suck at my job, but today, my heart swells with pride. I have strong, brave kids—all four of them.

An hour later, sitting with Jim, quietly talking to him and repeating my love mantra, I get a text from my brother. He's here, thank God! I need someone on my team guiding me through this, especially someone with Mike's EMT knowledge. I feel like I can breathe again, and like a little girl whose big brother is going to protect her at all costs. My vulnerability surfaces, and that thought makes me cry.

I meet Mike in the CCU waiting room, and when I take him back to see Jim, we find two paramedics in his room. I quickly deduce that when there's a close call, the men and women involved like to hear if the patient is going to make it. Thankfully, Jim is becoming more aware of his surroundings as the paralytic drug wears off. He nods to their questions, giving them a thumb's up. I move to his side and hold his hand, knowing he doesn't quite yet know what is happening around him.

In our relationship, I've always been the grounding force—which makes sense since I am an energy healer who's always striving to bring things into balance. Jim is the dreamer and schemer, the one who's always coming up with new ideas and fun projects, while I provide the ballast that helps bring them into reality. I hope I can hold my own and be that for him in this moment.

Mike is able to read the machines and explain what is happening. "It looks like Jim is receiving the best care possible," he says, "but as you probably know, Peg, most people don't survive coding three times. If you think of a computer shutting down and restarting several times, that's what his body did. And with all the CPR Jim received, he will have broken ribs, so just be forewarned that when he becomes more alert and the drugs wear off, he's gonna hurt like hell."

I don't want my husband to be in pain after such an ordeal, but I also know it's a welcome alternative to death.

I'll be there every step of the way to nurse him back to good health...just please let him live!

Mike leaves after assessing Jim's condition to go be Mr. Mom. I learn over text that he's quick to settle in with Landon, my baseball-playing kid, and watch the World Series. Landon asks questions about his dad, like what the tubes in his body are, and Mike is able to explain it to Landon's satisfaction before they're back to baseball and ice-cream sundaes. I breathe a sigh of relief that Mike is there for my son. Although my brother and I haven't been that close in recent years and he's not really familiar with my life and children, he seems to know intuitively what to do.

Jim is starting to become more alert by the hour. He's still uncomfortable but wanting some answers to questions like, "Where the hell am I, and what happened to me?" Since he still has a tube down his throat and is not able to talk, one of the nurses gets a pen and paper with a clipboard so Jim can write things down.

His first question is simple: "Pee?" The nurse explains he has a catheter in, so he can pee at will.

And then: "More air from the tube."

To clear blood and fluids out of the ventilator, they suction it. It is more horrific than helpful in my eyes, because it makes Jim gag so hard, it's like someone is lifting him off the bed.

Jim is clearly so desperate to breathe deep that he writes, "air suck." After they suction him, a plea: "I need time." I can sense he is overwhelmed, and if there is one thing I know about my husband above all else, he likes to be in control of himself and his surroundings.

Jim's day nurses, Becky and Tonya, work hard to keep him comfortable, but when the night nurse comes on at 7 p.m., I can feel in my gut that this is going to be a rough night. Jim is experiencing more pain and discomfort as the day progresses, and nothing is more disconcerting than a tube down your throat, with your hands tied down so you can't rip it out.

By 9 p.m. Jim is agitated and sore, and starting to feel everything, including the vent poking into the side of his throat. I know the night nurse is doing the best job possible, but part of the problem is that the pain meds are causing Jim's blood pressure to drop too low, so they can't give him enough to keep him comfortable. His body is starting to show signs of what he had been through only hours earlier. I look on in horror as his arms start turning a gross black-and-blue purple.

Jim writes down on his paper, "Can I cough? Hard to take a deep breath," followed by "Lot of work breathing. Little crunchy. Phlegm in lungs." The more alert Jim becomes, the look in his eyes quickly turns to terror, pain, and complete helplessness.

And then, there are the beeps. When they say that people don't sleep in hospitals, this is why. Every machine has an alarm. I am starting to feel nutty, but there is nothing to do but survive the next hour.

Jim writes on his paper, "Can I get more sleep? Meds wore off." I keep hitting the nurse call button to see if we can get Jim some relief. His pain and agitation are increasing rapidly. I can see by the look in his eyes that his pain is off the hospital scale of 1–10. I think he's at a 30!

I start wondering what happens to patients who have no one to be their advocate. Do they just lie there in intense fear and pain, wishing to die with no one to pull them out of it? It makes my heart break. Months later, Jim explains to me that throughout the whole night, he was watching the clock and willing himself to live just ten more minutes, just ten more minutes, all night long. He tells me that if I hadn't been there, he would have just willed himself to die.

It makes sense that people would have that kind of willpower. In my line of work I've heard stories from clients of loved ones who hang on so people flying in can say goodbye before they pass. Or timing their death to the moment someone who wants them to stay leaves the room.

Once again, I feel extremely grateful for my brother. Had he not flown in, I would have been torn between my children and my husband. Thank God I didn't have to make that call. At the same time, I question how helpful my presence is. Rather than being the peaceful eye at the center of the storm, I get more agitated as I see Jim's anxiety and unease increase. Nothing seems to be working as it should, and I am starting to lose it.

Three: Family

Technically it's been Thursday for hours now, but I have been lost in the swirl of trying to keep Jim alive. At 4:36 a.m., I text my brother: "F'ed-up night. Nurse couldn't get meds right, pretty awake and trying to rip ventilator out at 1 a.m. He's like a f-ing pincushion. I think I slept from 12 to 12:40 a.m."

Finally, at 5 a.m., an angel disguised as Dr. Hamden, an internal medicine doctor on duty, swoops in and asks what's happening.

Where did she come from? Where has she been the last four hours of hell?

"My husband is in pain and has been struggling to get comfortable all night," I tell her, exhausted and exasperated.

"I'm sorry to hear that, but to get patients off the ventilator, we need them to be coherent and awake— usually that means they feel a lot more pain as we reduce the meds. At this point, we will try and get him off the vent in the next few hours."

Dr. Hamden disappears as quickly as she came in. I feel relieved; this horrible night of pain and discomfort had a purpose, at least. It takes a couple more hours before they make the decision to extubate.

Dr. Abernathy, who is a hospitalist (a dedicated in-patient physician who works exclusively at a hospital), shows up at 7 a.m. and asks if I want to be in the room when she takes Jim's tube out.

"Uh no! Thank you, but no."

As I step out and take a short break, I breathe a sigh of relief. We're hitting a milestone here. If they feel Jim can breathe on his own then that means he is coming back from the brink!

Despite my relief, I feel like I've gone through hell and back. Thank God for Dr. Hamden, who was able to explain more clearly that they weren't being negligent. By reducing the pain meds and keeping his blood pressure stable, they were ensuring he could get off the ventilator. I have never been good at charades or guessing what my husband wants, so I know Jim will be happy to get the tube out so he can talk again.

Dr. Abernathy is on duty for most of Jim's stay. She is young, alert, and super intelligent. Jim and I quickly come to appreciate her knowledge and the fact that she gives us information and then lets us make choices based on that.

I can tell Jim likes her the minute she removes the breathing tube. (Side note: Someone should be able to invent something a lot less barbaric than a ventilator. The suctioning of the tube and how much it makes the patient gag is ungodly.) Dr. Abernathy also removes Jim's catheter, which he doesn't mind so much in comparison to the ventilator.

As I come back into the room, I hear Dr. Abernathy say, "I'm pleased that you're doing so well, Jim." I don't know how things typically progress with a patient in this situation, but I take this as a good sign. I am also happy to hear my husband's voice again. I know from my energy work that so much depends on how someone sounds. After all, your voice is related to your power. And if you can't speak up for yourself, you have none.

"My lungs feel chunky," Jim croaks out.

This makes sense, considering that they are still filled with clots. We won't see the CT scan until his first checkup with Dr. Young in January. It will show that, even after the tPA was administered, Jim's left lung was almost completely clogged and the right lung looked like it had chicken pox. The amount of blood clots that let loose into his lungs at that time was astounding.

Jim's first cough off the vent makes him realize just how bad his ribs hurt. Putting the pieces together now, I would imagine they did almost 45 minutes of continuous CPR on Jim. The paramedics explained that there was no way to *not* break ribs. When you think of a broken bone, you think of the bone split in two, but actually, broken ribs usually entail small cracks, or fissures, in the rib. This is why ribs take so long to heal—because all of those little fissures are knitting back together.

Just yesterday, I wanted Jim to wake up and talk to me. Now that he is fully awake and in a hell of a lot of pain, I realize the healing process has just begun.

Dr. Young stops in shortly after Dr. Abernathy leaves. Jim still hasn't officially met him, although he was intimately involved in the decision with Dr. Harwich to administer a full dose of tPA instead of using the IV drip. "It's so great to meet you, Jim," he says sincerely. "I'm glad you're still here with us."

Dr. Young goes on to say that he's amazed that Jim is alert and talking. "I was able to confirm that there was for sure a deep vein thrombosis that formed after the surgery on the left knee. Basically, small pieces of the DVT broke off and traveled through your bloodstream, Jim. Then they lodged in the arteries that supply the lungs."

A pulmonary embolism (PE) is a blockage to one of the lung's arteries. What Jim experienced yesterday was a massive pulmonary embolism. The PEs traveled up the veins in his leg, through the heart and into the lungs. Think of a clear highway that becomes blocked with cars; this is what Jim's lungs are like at this point. Besides the tPA dose, the doctors also put him on a heparin drip yesterday.

"Although the heparin will prevent any additional clotting from happening, it doesn't actually break down existing clots. Jim, to protect your heart and the rest of your body, we're going to put an inferior vena cava (IVC) filter down a vein in your neck," Dr. Young explains. "We have scheduled you for this procedure at 9:30 a.m., and it should be relatively quick."

Dr. Young goes on to explain that an IVC filter literally looks like a tiny umbrella that opens up inside your vein to collect the clots. Jim is pleased that there will be a layer of protection to prevent any more clots from traveling to his heart, lungs, or brain. He doesn't trust his body at all.

Dr. Young leaves, just as my friend Kelly texts to say she brought me breakfast and is in the CCU waiting room. I didn't realize how hungry I am and slip out to grab a quick bite. "Jim's family will be arriving in a couple of hours to relieve me." I explain to Kelly as I hug her goodbye. I am so grateful that Jim's parents and sisters didn't see him last night. His family members have the same attitude of strength and perseverance he has, which has served them well through life's up and downs. But I think seeing their son and brother on a ventilator clinging to life would have been too much. I certainly know I am not OK, and obviously, Jim is traumatized beyond words. He will tell me weeks from now, "I would rather die than be intubated again."

Meanwhile, at my house, given that he's on Montana time, my brother wakes my children up way too early with bugle horn revelry music. I get a text from my daughter Makenzie at 6:03 a.m.: "Jesus, Mike just woke us up with a bugle horn. Who is this man?"

Despite myself, I laugh. Mike and I were super close growing up. He was my big brother, my sun, moon, and stars. He is very kind and sensitive, and he would constantly rescue stray cats even though he was horribly allergic. We also shared a deep love of reading and the outdoors. (And, less happily, we ganged up on our baby sister and told her awful things, like she was adopted.) When both of us got married and had children, he moved from Kirkland to Montana, and we slowly grew apart.

Although I feel fortunate that he's here, I would have never expected him to jump on a plane and fly to my rescue.

It makes me reconsider the assumptions I made about Mike and our relationship. Maybe we were closer than I'd actually thought, and I was wrong for not tending our connection the way I used to. Whatever the case, having him show up at the CCU in my time of need has told me everything I needed to know. Whatever tension might have been in the air between us previously has gone poof.

My mom calls to let me know that she and my dad left Ritzville, Washington (about two-and-a-half hours away), early and are close to Kirkland. After dropping their stuff off at Aunt Peggy's house, they will be right up. I feel myself relax even more. My parents are salt-of-the-earth people. They love to help their friends, neighbors, and whoever crosses their path and asks for it. When I was a kid, my mother was an avid PTA mom who had been involved with the governor's War on Drugs campaign. My dad was a teacher who loved to do construction on the side.

It would never have occurred to my parents to just get on a plane and fly out to be with us. However, as I was hashing out the logistics in my head over the last several hours, I realized we would need their car and their services to shuttle Jim's family to and from the hospital and carpooling the kids to school. Given their helpful nature, I know they will do whatever I ask.

I giggle as I see another text from Makenzie at 7:07 a.m. It turns out that Mike dropped the kids off a little too early. "I'm at school, and the door to the high school is locked. I repeat, who is this man?"

After Jim gets the ventilator out at 7:30 a.m., I sit quietly next to him and can sense we are both decompressing from all that has happened since yesterday. It hasn't even been 24 hours since his collapse. My brother interrupts our stolen moment texting me to let me know he is in the CCU waiting room with my parents, who he picked up after dropping off my kids.

Jim nods for me to go meet them and I am swept up in a wonderful Mom hug. "We tried to get here as soon as we could, honey. We flew out of the restaurant so fast, we didn't realize that your dad left his coat at the restaurant we'd been eating at when you called!"

Tears come to my eyes when I learn they drove as far and as fast as they could yesterday, then woke up early this morning to finish the ten-hour journey from Montana to get to me.

I bring my parents in to see Jim. They also have tears in their eyes, which makes my own start pouring down my cheeks. A nurse interrupts our cry fest and announces, "I'm going to take Jim for his procedure now. I'll let you know when he's done."

We return to the waiting room and I can see my parents look exhausted. Mike decides to take them to Aunt Peggy's house to do some work and rearrange his schedule. He got here so fast yesterday, I am sure he left his work in the lurch.

Jim is in and out of his IVC filter procedure in 15 minutes. I've never seen a man so happy to get an umbrella put in his vein. I am grateful for the surgery, even though I am told that blood clots don't just disappear overnight, even with an anticoagulant drug.

For years, my husband thought he had the power to tell his body to behave and didn't believe anything would ever be majorly wrong with him. Sure he drank wine (which, of course, he had read is good for you), but he didn't smoke, and had a fairly decent diet of organic meats, fruits, and vegetables. His only two unhealthy vices: potato chips and pizza.

"I'm terrified," he admits to me as I sit and hold his hand. It's nice to have a quiet moment of connection.

Yesterday, he'd felt so far away from me. As a couple, we have our own circle of intimacy, and then yesterday, the whole world was inside of it. Now we are back to the two of us. Jim adds, "I don't like being out of control, and feeling this pressure in my chest."

I don't want him to see that I'm also scared, so I focus on any details that will help me understand what he needs to heal. "Do you remember anything, from the moment you…" I don't want to say the word "coded," but I don't have to.

He thinks for a moment. "Not really. I told you I loved you. Then, everything just faded to black. I took a dirt nap. No seeing the light. Nothing, just darkness."

Near-death experiences (NDEs) fascinate me, so I am secretly disappointed he didn't hear angels singing, or "see the light" as I had heard from a few of my clients who experienced NDEs. I know that he doesn't want to hear about the details of yesterday, that he only wants to move on, so I try to comfort him with other things: the kids' lives, and the fact that his parents will be arriving soon. He is tired from his ordeal and nods off while I am talking.

It becomes clear that the CCU doesn't want to keep Jim here too long. All of their efforts are focused on freeing him from the machines he's hooked up to. Although he's off the respirator, he is still on oxygen because his lungs are still filled with blood clots. Jim got a local anesthetic for his procedure to keep him comfortable, so he has an opportunity to rest after a horrible night and wait for his parents to show up.

Their plane will be landing soon. Logan is picking them up and bringing them straight to the hospital. Jim's parents find it too hard to drive when they don't know where they are going, and it's probably better for all of us that they don't.

Logan texts me when they get to the hospital so I can meet them in the CCU waiting room, which has quickly become a second home. When I see his normally youthful parents, for the first time they look their real ages. I hug them both. I'm also happy to see that Jodie and Bunnie, Jim's two sisters, are here. Bunnie has a fear of flying, and the last time she came out to Seattle was for our wedding.

"You two decided to come!" I exclaim. "I'm so glad you're here."

"We had to come see our brother," Jodie says, her voice choked with emotion.

"We're here until Monday to help out," Bunnie adds, squeezing my hand briefly. "Just tell us what we need to do."

(Yes, his mom really goes by Cookie, and his sister by Bunnie. They're both named Linda, but it's been Cookie and Bunnie forever.)

"How is my son?" Carlos asks.

"I'll let you see for yourself," I say, quickly ushering them into Jim's room.

When they see Jim in his hospital bed, Carlos breaks down. "My son, my son," he exclaims in anguish. Feeling like I am intruding on a private moment, I step out quietly into the hall and go brief Jodie and Bunnie on Jim's current state and what he has been through. Given how much has transpired, it feels good to talk about it and work through the details with other people.

All of Jim's female family members are nurses, and they quickly get up to speed on the severity of the situation. So, between Mike's EMT knowledge and the nursing know-how of Jim's family, everyone's insight is golden. Jodie and Bunnie go into Jim's room next, trading off with their parents, which gives me a chance to talk with them. I love them like my own parents.

I can tell that they are distressed, so I try to reassure Carlos and Cookie. "We're through the worst of it. Dr. Young felt that the first 24-hour mark after the tPA was administered was the most crucial, and we are definitely past that point."

Jim's parents stay a couple hours before going back to our house to sleep. Bunnie and Jodie remain, and we take turns humoring Jim all afternoon to take his mind off his pain. What Jim's family doesn't lack is comic relief, so we hear all sorts of hilarious family stories that hopefully serve as distractions for my husband.

The hospital had put Jim on a heparin drip shortly after the tPA dose was administered. My understanding is that the tPA was used to stop another cardiac arrest and break up the DVT, and the heparin will prevent and treat blood clots. They have to titrate the heparin, meaning they must continuously measure and adjust the dosage. One of the nurses tells me, "We're still worried about the possibility that Jim might have internal bleeding."

This means they have to draw blood every one to two hours and check Jim's hematocrit (blood volume) level. On top of that, the heparin isn't without its long list of side effects, including but not limited to bloody urine, unusual bruising, extreme fatigue, nausea, bone pain, fever, and sudden difficulty speaking or understanding speech.

I frown when I hear the list. Given my own background as a healer, I struggle with the discrepancies between Eastern and Western medicine. Clearly, I understand that Jim needs doctors and medical intervention, but to what degree?

Logan, our oldest, has a neurological disease, so we are familiar with the medical world. Logan's health challenges shaped our choices about healthcare for all of our children, and nudged me into my current profession as an Energy Healer in my attempt to seek answers to best help my son.

Jim and I have always leaned toward a holistic health approach, which includes a focus on good nutrition, supplements as needed, and chiropractic, acupuncture, and massage as additions. So, while I'm not too enthused that Jim is being pumped full of drugs, in his case it's necessary. Jim would not be alive right now without Western medicine.

I feel deep compassion for the nurses and doctors who are kept on their toes by the imperative to save all the people who come their way. With my own work, I am helping people heal their emotional and spiritual aspects, but the people in this hospital are healers in their own right, healing people's physical bodies. Despite some of my own doubts about the medical model, I recognize that we actually have a lot in common—for one thing, our optimism in the systems we've subscribed to, no matter how different they might seem on the surface.

Day has slowly slipped into night and Jim can see that I am exhausted. "Why don't you go home and get some sleep and see the kids, honey?" Jim asks.

I hesitate, happy that Jim has passed the 24 hour mark where the danger of him bleeding to death was high, but still trying to shake the image of him lying in our front hallway.

"You sure? I love seeing you in immense pain with massively purple arms," I tease, as I gently lean in to kiss his cheek. "I'm going to miss all the beeps and people sticking you every hour."

Jim laughs quietly so as not to aggravate his ribs or start a coughing fit. We have always used humor to lighten the mood when our lives get too intense.

"We can spend the night here with Jim," Jodie assures me, settling into the chair that was my "bed" the night before.

I head out with one more goodbye to Jim and find my car in the parking lot after a few clicks of my key fob. Driving a car feels strange now, like I've been on a long vacation or a protracted out-of-body experience. Now, here I am, a normal human just driving my car home for the night. At least, I'm sure that's how I look to the other drivers on the road.

I let out a deep breath I've been holding in since yesterday, and reflect for a moment how drastically life can change in the blink of an eye. One minute I was going to work, the next I'm in a hospital. I'm amazed that I've been able to keep up with all that's happened, especially since I don't understand half the words the doctors have relayed to me. Add some sleep deprivation and exhaustion to that mix, and it is quite the cocktail.

As I pull into my garage, I start to cry. I'm back home, but this is also the scene of Jim's CPR event, where this entire nightmare began. I am not left alone in my grief for too long. As soon as I get in the door, I am greeted with hugs as my kids gather around me, screaming, "Mom!"

I put down my computer bag and wrap Landon, my youngest, in my arms. "Hi sweetie, I've missed you." I can smell delicious odors wafting from the kitchen, which makes me remember that Cookie is an excellent cook. I smile to myself, knowing that the kids are in good hands.

Cookie quickly ushers me into the kitchen. "You're here just in time for dinner!" She still has circles under her eyes, and I know she's probably about as emotionally exhausted as I am. But I'm guessing that taking care of my family gives her a purpose that helps take her mind off Jim's condition.

Over dinner, I catch the kids up on everything that's happened. "I don't want you to freak out, but I am going to have to stay at the hospital. No promises, but I'll come home as much as I can. That means you're going to need to hang in there and take care of each other. And, of course, Grandma and Grandpa are here for you." The kids all nod. They know that my main job is to help their dad heal and get home. And at this point, there's no timeline for that.

Our motto for our house is, "Practice loving kindness." Over the years, they've teased me for it and called me Oprah, but clearly, love makes a difference. After all, what do we cling to in a crisis? People who love us, and love us unconditionally. Everything in my life at this point is a testament to that. All of our friends and family who love me, Jim, and the kids matter so much.

After spending a little more time with my kids, I crawl up to bed. My heart practically stops when I see the front hallway rug with Jim's blood still on it. Momentarily, I am taken back to when it all happened.

Keep it together, Peg.

I can tell from the way I am twitching and shaking that I am in shock. Landon grabs my hand. "Are you OK, Mom?" he asks, concern in his eyes. I don't remember what I say, but I know that Landon knows I'm upset.

"I'm going to sleep on Dad's side of the bed tonight, OK?" he says, although it's more of a statement than a question. I'm grateful for my son's presence, but I don't want him to see me like this. I want to be the one who protects him, not the other way around. At the same time, nothing can be done. Just like their mom, my kids are intuitive. Landon recognizes that something in me has shifted.

Four: Healer

I wake up from a decent night of sleep, early, as usual. I realize the kids have to get to school. *How is that going to happen?* I wonder.

I smile as I look at Landon, who's curled up in bed next to me. I gently nudge him, "Honey, it's time to get ready for school!" I say.

He opens his eyes slowly, then greets me with a smile. "Morning, Mom, can I have a hug?"

I hug him tightly and ruffle his hair. Landon is a bright light in this world, and his belly laugh is one of my favorite sounds. I feel so grateful for my sensitive, inquisitive 11-year-old. His love for Jim is all-encompassing, given the fact that not only do they share an appreciation of all things sports (baseball and golf being at the top of the list), but a zest for life, as well. Both tease and laugh constantly. Landon is always game for anything, so Jim loves to come up with adventures and projects they can share together. And although Jim can be stubborn, Landon balances him out with his sweetness.

A momentary storm cloud interrupts my moment of peace, as I think of what it would mean for Landon to lose his dad...especially at this age. *He's already been through too much in just the last 48 hours*, I think to myself.

There were many unspoken words and emotions in that look we exchanged last night: his pain, my pain, him witnessing my pain. How could I unwind what he had seen? I know I can't and that part of being a Mom is helping him grow and learn from the hard times, not just the good ones.

My life is deeply intertwined with each of my children, their heartaches, struggles, what their friends are doing, where they are in their own worlds. The fun of having four children is they are all unique and beautiful in their own ways. I hear Makenzie, age 16, get up and go to the bathroom in the hall. I smile to myself. It's nice to be back in my morning routine of waking kids up.

Madison, my older daughter, is 18. This is her senior year of high school, a big year with lots of activities, and we are also in the middle of applying to colleges and getting her final applications in. I am excited, albeit apprehensive, to see what her future holds.

I realize I don't hear Madison stirring in her room, so I yell downstairs, "Madison, are you up?" To my surprise, I hear a faint "yes." Most mornings, I drag her out of bed because she is not an early riser. Now that Jim isn't driving, she has a car to drive herself to school. To do that, though, you must be awake. I'm happy she's up and leaving soon.

Not wanting to get up, I sink deeper into my cocoon of blankets and think about my oldest son, Logan. He was only four months old when we discovered that he might have neurofibromatosis 1 (NF1). It's a relatively rare disease, affecting approximately 1 in 4,000 people in the U.S. Around 30% of the time, it shows up as a spontaneous occurrence, like it did in Logan's case, but it is usually passed on through genetics.

The doctors explained to us it's a "wait and see" disease so it wasn't until age nine that he was firmly diagnosed when he developed lisch nodules on his eyes. The disease is a real pain in the ass, and Logan has endured a lot in his short life. NF1 is tumor-based, so the goal is to have a low-stress life, a non-inflammatory diet, and low impact on one's bones and joints. He developed a brain tumor at age 12, or what they call an optic glioma. It just sits on his optic chiasm with the risk that if it grows, Logan could lose his sight. So far, so good.

Logan's diagnosis is another reason why I started my healing journey. My anxiety around "wait and see" prompted me to think of other ways of healing the body and taking his situation into my own hands. The years leading up to his firm diagnosis had been challenging, but through it all, I'd been proactive about finding other "remedies" for his situation, ranging from acupuncture to chiropractic, and speech and occupational therapy.

I was determined to heal my son, so I quickly threw out my old belief that if you were sick, you went to the doctor and they fixed it. I needed to think outside the box in Logan's case. I pull myself out of my musings and steer Landon in the direction of my bathroom. "Get clean and then head downstairs, I'll shower after you."

I lay my head back on the pillow, thinking back to what finally pushed me into healing school, besides Logan's NF1. I got swept up into my role as a mom raising four little kids, with no awareness, boundaries or ability to take care of myself. My whole life was my family, husband, and children. I was living what I would now call "unconsciously."

This led to my own health crisis in July 2001, when Makenzie was a baby. Because I lacked self-care I was horribly sick her entire pregnancy resulting in a tonsillectomy when she was five months old. All good until I hemorrhaged thirteen days post op. What I remember from that time was the thought "*I won't live to see 40 if I continue down this path*".

Knowing what I know now, rock bottom is when we finally seek help, and I had reached mine! Help only came five years later, in the form of my four-year healing school that had the benign description of teaching you Earth energy healing, with no mention of personal process work.

By this time, I was a much healthier human and had given my body four years to heal before having my fourth and final child at the age of 34. My first day in class, my instructor, Alima (ah-lEE-muh) looked us square in the eyes and said, "Throw out everything you have been told you are by others, because it is a lie. Every single one of you is here to discover your true self."

Oh shit, I thought to myself. *What have you signed up for here, Peg?*

I had been slow on the uptake, but I knew I was doing life "wrong," and that it was time to try a different tactic. Prior to this, I didn't even know what it meant to operate from my intuition, but that was about to change.

The first two years were rough, and I wanted to quit every day. Alima wasn't exactly easy on me. She routinely told me, "You're in denial, and you have to start stepping up and getting the answers you need for Logan—and yourself."

By year three of healing school, I was finally starting to believe in myself and was ready to share my knowledge with others. It took me until year four to gather the courage to open up my own healing practice. My 39th birthday present to myself was opening my business, Soul Window. Jim was my first and only client that day, but it was a start.

More than anything, my experience with healing school and creating my own practice opened me to all kinds of alternative healing methods and taught me to empower others to change their situations. It also introduced me to a new community of people who felt the same way.

My thoughts are interrupted when Logan pops his head in the door and asks, "Mom, what do you need today?"

"I won't know until I get back up to the hospital," I say. "How are you holding up sweetie?"

He pauses before he responds, "I'm not able to eat much and I feel like I'm still in shock...but work is a nice distraction."

I sigh, glad for his strength, but also concerned. "I'm working to find you a therapist." I say, getting out of bed and giving him a giant hug. "I love you so much. You were so brave Wednesday morning!"

Logan smiles at me before he goes off to shower to get ready for work. Landon comes out of my bathroom, finished with his shower, and I go in to continue what we call "the shower train."

As the hot water washes over me, I realize I don't want the trauma of what has happened to Jim to stick to my son. Right now, Logan and I are displaying all the signs of trauma survivors: lack of sleep, irritability, anger, anxiety, and hypervigilance. On top of that, Logan has had headaches and isn't able to eat much.

After a short shower, I quickly dress, dry my hair, and head downstairs to eat with Landon. Carlos is up and has cooked breakfast for all of us. "Thank you for this," I tell him. We are midway through our meal when Cookie joins us in the kitchen.

I know that Jim's parents had been debating going back to Boston on Monday with Jodie and Bunnie. If I am at the hospital 24/7 with Jim, I don't know what I'll do without my in-laws in the house.

"Please stay and help me!" I plead. "I'm not strong enough to do this on my own."

Cookie gives me a hug and doesn't hesitate. "Of course we'll stay! We'll help out with anything you need: for Jim or the kids. We're here for you, Peg."

I'm worried about the stress this situation is putting on Jim's parents. but I just don't know who else is free to take care of a family for a month. Healing school taught me to ask for help.

Getting a glimpse of what it could be like to be a single mom, I quickly push away the thought of being a widow at age 45.

My parents arrive at 6:45 a.m. to take Makenzie and Landon to school. They tell me that they'll come to the hospital after that to bring Jodie and Bunnie back to my house. Having said goodbye to my kids and making sure that my other family members are taken care of, I gather an overnight bag and a blanket (hospitals are cold) and head back up to Evergreen.

"Hi, honey."

I stop in the doorway, stunned that the sexy whisper voice is coming from Jim.

Jodie answers the question forming in my head. "So basically, Jim coughed the hell out of his lungs all night and lost his voice." Despite myself, I laugh.

Bunnie explains, "That's actually good for clearing the clots, but with his fractured ribs and tender ventilator throat? Not so great."

Although he's still hooked up to all kinds of machines, he looks much better than yesterday. I'm glad to see that a night nurse had made him a makeshift pillow to clutch to his chest when he coughed, hopefully easing some of the pain. Jim has high anxiety, and this situation has clearly put him over the top. Jodie said they worked out a system to get through the night. Every time he'd cough, Jodie would say, "Good one," and Bunnie would tell Jim his current oxygen level and heart rate.

Naturally, Jim no longer trusts his body, or has any clue what's going on inside of it. Will his lungs recover? Will his oxygen levels drop to 20 again? Is his heart damaged? It had stopped three times—could it really come back from that?

Like everyone else, I don't have answers to any of these questions. I am just in the trenches trying to help him survive the day. My parents arrive and take Jodie and Bunnie home to our house to sleep. Jim and I take a minute to reconnect and talk about his current status.

We hold hands, and I can sense how tired he is. I think he's still in shock from his collapse. If you've ever been really ill, you will understand what it's like when you have no energy to even know or ask for what you need. He has that look as he whispers, "I know you had to go home last night, but I really didn't like not having you here. I need you."

When you've been in an intimate relationship for 25 years, you have your own language. I get what he's saying without him having to say it. A sister is different from a wife, and he doesn't want to insult Jodie and Bunnie, but he needs me there to read his unspoken cues and be his rock and advocate.

"I understand," I say. "I felt like it was important to check in with the kids last night. They still don't fully understand what happened to you, and I really needed sleep. They had two highly engaged parents—and now they have zero. I promise to stay with you until you're discharged, and I'll just go home for showers."

"It was impossible to sleep last night, I was coughing so hard." Jim whispers. "My sisters are great, but I just want *you*."

Tonya is back as the day nurse and comes into the room. I can see that she is on a mission. Jim is no longer considered to be in critical condition, so he'll soon be graduating to a new part of the hospital. Given his unique case, they spend the day trying to figure out what floor he belongs on and find him a bed. In the meantime, Tonya works with Jim to help him re-engage with daily tasks. First up: a move from the bed to the chair.

You would have thought Jim ran a full marathon, given how labored his breathing is and how much his oxygen has dipped. I know Jim is scared by how little his body is functioning, and even though I'm trying to remain calm, it scares the shit out of me, too.

Every time I think of how dire his situation is, new layers of understanding are formed. It would be one thing if just his lungs were compromised by the clots. But add to that the fact he died three times, all of his organs shut down and restarted, his heart went through three cardiac arrests, his knee still needs rehab, he has a giant DVT in his leg, all the CPR had fractured his ribs (the worst pain imaginable), and the ventilator had damaged his throat, which is now being exacerbated by the cough. As he moves from bed to chair, I realize that this isn't going to be a two-week ordeal; it might take Jim six months to a year to heal from all he's been through. I sigh as I let that sink in.

"Can you sit in the chair, Jim?" Tonya asks, bringing a basin, a cup of water, a toothbrush, and toothpaste so that he can brush his teeth.

"I think so," Jim wheezes as he sits up. He winces from rib pain but brushes his teeth. He looks like a little boy, delicate and fragile. I want to hug him, but everything is too tender. Next, Tonya hands Jim wipes and instructs him: "Wash your face and neck. Just be careful of the liquid bandage from the IVC filter."

"Here, let me help you," I say as I grab the wipes. "You're all orange from the iodine they used to clean your neck for surgery." I remove as much orange dye as I can, and then discover Jim still has the sticky pads on his chest from the defibrillator.

"Take a deep breath," I say and rip them off.

"Nothing like a free chest hair wax," Jim jokes through his grimace.

His parents walk in a few minutes later. "Looking good, Sonny Boy!" Carlos happily exclaims, as Cookie comes over to give him a gentle pat on his arm. "Nice to see you out of bed!"

At around 3:30 p.m., we are official graduates of the CCU. Jim's parents and I follow the aide, who wheels Jim across the hospital to his new digs. I gasp when I see them. We've gone from what they call the CCU fishbowl to the penthouse. Jim is now in a corner room in the "silver tower" on the medical/surgery eighth floor.

I'm happy to see how much space Jim now has—perfect for visits from his large family. My girlfriend, Maureen dropped Jodie and Bunnie back off at the hospital and they are grateful we can all be in Jim's room together. At this point, Jim's prognosis hasn't been made clear to us and we still don't know how long he's going to be here.

The nurses work to get Jim settled in a much more comfortable bed, bundling him up with warm blankets. He is peeing blood, which signals internal bleeding from somewhere. The doctors are concerned, and there are phlebotomists coming to take blood every couple hours and monitor his blood volume. It has been slowly dropping, which is also raising red flags. A normal hematocrit level is 40, and Jim is down to a 32. When you drop to a 22, they start transfusions.

I am quickly given the title of "Peg Wife" on the eighth floor. Jim's medicines, as well as the conditions that changed in the past day and the names of the nurses assigned to him at any given moment, are on a whiteboard on the wall. The board quickly becomes my daily anchor. My brain is becoming fuzzier and fuzzier the longer I go without sleep, and I need a clear picture of what's going on without being inundated by "doctor speak."

With Jim happily ensconced in the penthouse that afternoon, I take his parents and Bunnie home with me and leave Jodie with my husband. "I'll do the night shift with you," she'd told me earlier.

For now, I want to spend a couple hours with my kids and bring Makenzie back up to say goodbye to her dad. She is leaving for a couple of days on a pre-planned trip.

Our neighbors had seen the flurry of emergency vehicles two days ago and texted me earlier to ask if they could bring a meal over. Of course, I said yes. One of the first things that goes out the window when you're in the midst of a trauma is your ability to cook and plan for meals. As important as it is, it's the last thing on your mind. I've never had a big appetite in times of difficulty, so I ask for a simple meal: roast chicken, broccoli, and potatoes.

Gathered around the dinner table with my family as we talk about our days, I feel a moment of contentment.

My kids have rallied in the last 48 hours, getting themselves to school and their activities with a lot of help from friends and family. As they talk to me, I can sense how strong they are. We joke as a family that if you can't find something, don't know something, or need help, ask Mom. She just magically knows where everything is, can solve any problem, or get you the information you need to solve it. I can tell in our current situation that they have gone back to their normal routines and have utter faith that Mom will solve this problem, too. She needs to save their dad, be his advocate, and make sure that everyone is doing their job when it comes to his care. Because he isn't out of the woods yet, there's no room for error.

That evening, I bring Makenzie back to the hospital to visit her dad. I can tell that she's pleased to see how much has changed over the last two days.

"Hey," Jim greets our daughter.

"Dad, you're talking!" Even though it's more of a whisper.

We spend a little time together, talking about both the minutiae and big stuff in our lives. Almost like we're having a normal family conversation. After that, I leave Jodie with Jim to drive Makenzie to the airport.

The to and from the hospital gives me time to be with myself and reflect on all that has happened in two days. A wave of gratitude washes over me. Jim is still alive. The tiredness then settles into my bones. I actually honor it, and I stop to thank my body for all of its hard work.

Please be strong for me. And keep going.

I sigh, recognizing that all of the healing work I have been doing with my clients these last seven years has prepared me for this challenge. I inhale and exhale a few deep breaths as I pull back up to the hospital, ready to face what comes next.

The nights are by far the worst for Jim, and I am happy I have Jodie with me. When the dark of night moves in, his anxiety goes through the roof. Something about everything going black kicks up a fear that he may not live to see the morning.

"I don't think that the nurses and doctors in charge of your care would let you die in the hospital, love," I tell him, trying to be reassuring while inserting a dose of sarcasm. "Usually, the whole point is for them to help you heal."

That's when Makenzie texts me from the airport at 10:58 p.m.

"What color is Dad's aura?"

My kids think it's fascinating that their mom is an energy healer who can see colors and auras, and they like to know how it works. I have been trained as a hands-on healer to run energy from the Earth through my system, but I'm also a Reiki Master who can work remotely. I typically see through my "third eye," or the sixth chakra—which is the energetic center from which we interpret intuitive messages.

"It's like a movie is rolling through and I get images, colors, flashes of what a person's field is doing," I usually explain to people. When I do hands-on healing, I am most accurate about my intuitive hits.

After reading Makenzie's text, I hold Jim's feet and let myself be a conduit for Earth energy until the images start flashing through.

I text Makenzie an answer: "Dad's aura is fractured."

It's strange...despite the seven years of work I've done as an energy healer, and the four years I spent in healing school, in the past couple days, I have only peripherally thought about how my knowledge can help Jim heal. Prompted by my daughter's text, this is the first time I start considering what I can do for my husband— from an esoteric vantage point. I have been so in the moment, I have forgotten who I am.

When I first opened my practice, Alima told me, "Peg, just remember that you don't shut down your healing abilities once you leave your office."

Duh. It's not just my job. *I'm a healer 24/7.*

Remembering that I have a window of insight into Jim's condition that not everyone does, I feel slightly exhilarated.

After all, I *know* what to do with a fractured aura.

Five: Surrender

Last night Makenzie's text woke me up to what is most important.

I need to heal my husband.

That's it. Everything else has to be put on the back burner until he is healed.

In reading Jim's energy field, I realized that he had reacted to the trauma of coding multiple times by fracturing his auric field into pieces. Our energy, or auric, field is a very subtle layer of protection around the physical body. Think of it like an eggshell around an egg. There are seven layers of the field that I am trained to sense, manipulate, or repair. Reading a field is like reading a book: You are scanning the layers of the field, just like skimming the pages of a book. A lot of energy work entails using your imagination and holding a clear intention for the highest good, however in my training we were taught clear healing techniques for situations like this.

I close my eyes and get a clear picture of Jim in my mind. Then I "ask" to see his first layer. I have a continual conversation with Spirit while I work. I've learned I can ask questions and, *surprise*, I get answers. I move methodically through the layers, starting with the first up to the seventh layer. The first three layers, reflecting our connection to Earth, seem tight and constricted. The fourth layer is the astral plane or a place in your field where you connect to the spiritual realms; I can't seem to see where this layer is at the moment, almost as if Jim is questioning his connection to the Earth plane and floating in the astral.

The fifth layer is the Divine plan, and this is where I see the fracturing, which then has a cascading effect on the lower layers. I also notice that Jim's sixth and seventh layers are *huge* in comparison to the first five. This makes sense, as the sixth layer represents our connection to the angelic realms, and the seventh is connection to God. Even though Jim didn't "see the light," I think he has been spending a lot of the last three days in the spiritual world.

In other words, not *here*.

I can see that Jim needs help bringing the pieces back in. However, this has to be his choice. I know if I force my an agenda for Jim's healing on him, I can cause a psychic break or a permanent splitting off from his auric field entirely. The last thing I want to do is jam him full of energy with the idea of fixing him and then recreate the trauma of yesterday.

Jim's energetic reaction trauma is a common one. He disconnected from the Earth plane and split his energy field into pieces to protect himself. That sounds counter-intuitive: How does splitting into pieces actually protect you? The answer is, there is less of you available for the trauma to stick to.

The best example I have of this is sexual abuse victims. Sometimes, they break into little pieces during the abuse and then come back together later. As I've discovered in my practice, while the breaking apart early on is a survival mechanism, later they will need help finding and gathering those pieces of their field back together to become truly whole and well. Otherwise, they will always be in the field of their trauma.

I remind myself now of one of the first steps of healing: Surrender to the fact that this is *Jim's* healing journey. I am just here to hold sacred space for him to move through it as gracefully as possible, without imposing my desire to speed up that process or fix things for him.

OK, done.

In order to be of any use to my husband, I must become a fluid conduit of energy. That's the only way I can put Jim's energy field back together—and the only way I can save him.

I learned all of these energetic nuances and skills when I attended the Northwest School of Healing for four years from November of 2006 to June of 2010. There is something that happens when you start doing energy work: I call it "the shift." What was once your internal frame of reference is no more. It's like you begin seeing the world through a different lens. It's disconcerting at first, but ultimately, it's liberating.

When I started the healing school, I did not have a sense of myself or my true power. Most of us are bobbing along this wave called life pretty comfortably until someone challenges us with questions like: *Who are you, really, beyond who you think you are?*

To tell the truth, I didn't know. I'd defined myself on the basis of being a mom and wife, and all the struggles with Logan's health, as well as my own, had left little time or inclination for deeper self-reflection.

For years, Julie, my neighbor and friend, would constantly nudge me. "Peg, you don't do anything for yourself," she would chide.

I would wave her off like a fly. "I have the kids, and I'm wrapped up in helping them."

I truly didn't understand how bad I was at taking care of myself, asking for help and finding balance in my life. When I got pregnant with Logan, our first child, Jim and I went over the finances and realized that my entire paycheck would go to child care, so why not just quit my job and stay home to raise our kids? It was an easy decision, but I confess I didn't know what I was signing up for. I was 26 years old when I had Logan, and then I quickly had my next two children. Landon came a little bit later because of my health challenges.

Julie had children who were the same ages as mine, but she approached motherhood differently. She didn't seem as lost in her role as I did.

"Stop over at 4 p.m. and have a glass of wine," Julie would say.

"No thanks," was always my reply.

I wasn't connecting the dots that you had to maintain a sense of yourself as a woman, and you just don't give up your power and sacrifice everything for your children. Throughout our friendship, she had seen me go from a mom of three kids to now four, all under the age of eight. I would go out occasionally with girlfriends, but I didn't have a healthy day-to day-balance. Naturally, Julie was concerned for my well-being.

"Peg, I think you should go to my healing school," Julie told me.

"What's that?" I asked.

"You learn techniques to heal yourself and others, and to connect to your truth more deeply. You'll love it—I know it's totally your thing," Julie encouraged.

"I don't even understand energy healing, and when would I have time for it?" I asked, scarcely believing she'd suggest such a thing.

"You have to *make* the time," she replied, as if it were the most obvious thing in the world.

To silence her, I agreed to go to a weekend hands-on healing workshop in the spring of 2006. It was like a first date. I felt something stirring inside of me, like this could be the thing that would finally help me find myself…but with four small kids at home, I wouldn't even think to ask Jim if I could go. I just assumed his answer was going to be a firm no.

Julie wore me down over time with her persistence: "Peg, you have to take yourself into account, so please go to the school."

"Peg the school starts in two months, and Alima agrees you should be there."

"Peg, get off your butt and go!"

I was like a little kid with my hands over my ears. "Nah, nah, nah, not listening." I'm surprised she kept at me. She even had her friend Kelly, who is now a close friend of mine, call me: "Peg, you don't know me, but Julie and I know you are meant to be at the healing school. We agree with Alima that this is where you need to be, even if *you* can't see it."

Julie had a quote in her room that she'd picked up at the healing school. It was by Marianne Williamson, and I loved it:

"Our deepest fear is not that we are inadequate. Our deepest fear is that we are powerful beyond measure. It is our light, not our darkness, that most frightens us. We ask ourselves, Who am I to be brilliant, gorgeous, talented, and fabulous? Actually, who are you not to be? You are a child of God. Your playing small does not serve the world. There's nothing enlightened about shrinking so that other people won't feel insecure around you. We were born to make manifest the glory of God that is within us. It's not just in some of us; it's in everyone. And as we let our own light shine, we unconsciously give other people permission to do the same. As we are liberated from our own fear, our presence automatically liberates others."

After six months of Julie heckling me about attending the healing school, I thought, *OK universe, she's not letting up; if I am meant to go, give me a sign.* The next morning, I ripped off my day calendar and found these words: "Our deepest fear is not that we are inadequate. Our deepest fear is that we are powerful beyond measure. It is our light, not our darkness, that most frightens us."

It was hard to ignore that sign, so that was the day I signed up for healing school.

Sadly, shortly after I started, my beautiful friend Julie was diagnosed with a rare form of liver cancer. We had many raw, real conversations during my first two years of school, while she was dying, and she would always tell me, "Peg, you're going to hang a shingle out in the world. I know you're going to be an amazing healer."

I am still moved to tears thinking of how much faith she had in me. Although, I lost my friend, her death only accelerated my own healing and desire to get real about myself and my shortcomings.

Just as I'd predicted, Jim and I fought about me going to the school. "This is crazy!" he'd exclaimed. "You're a mom of four kids, and you want to spend two weekends a month and two nights a week away from them?"

It was a big sacrifice for all of us. That, and it challenged all of our belief systems. I had never heard of energy healers, and yet here I was embarking on a journey to become one. The most alternative practitioner we saw was a chiropractor, and only because Logan developed scoliosis, another side effect of the NF1. There were many times when I contemplated throwing in the towel and giving up, but for some reason, I couldn't put the idea down. Julie's words stuck with me. And in my heart of hearts, I knew I needed to save me from me. I knew my body, mind, and spirit were *tired*.

I was angry at Jim for having the freedom of going to work and doing as he pleased all day. I felt like I got duped when I signed on to stay at home and raise our children. I wanted to rewrite my contract. Looking back now, I can say those were the hardest years of our marriage. I was an angry, tired, overworked mom, all because of my lack of self-care, love, and respect for myself.

The first two years of healing school were all about self-examination and getting to the core of our being and what we are all about. It felt like I was turning myself inside out...it was excruciating. In the process, I had to face some pretty ugly truths about myself. For instance, I had a huge victim complex, I was passive aggressive, and I avoided conflict at all costs. I had no idea how to ask for what I needed to support my inner desires, because I didn't want to be told "no." I had to carefully examine all my flaws and recognize that, in order to be a free conduit of healing energy, I needed to get out of my own way.

The hardest moments were when Alima challenged me. "Peg, you're in complete denial of what is going on with your family and children," she told me one day. I don't think I responded; I just silently cursed at her in my head and then started to cry.

As harsh as she sounded, it jarred something deep within, and I knew she was right. I wanted to paint this picture of this perfect wife, kids, and family for the outside world, but I was painting myself into a corner where none of that was true. I was like a zombie going through the motions. My life was a glossy picture that had no depth or meaning. I wasn't living in the present, enjoying every second. I was just marching through each day without feeling anything.

Once you pull on the threads of the tapestry of your life that you have woven, they start to unravel pretty quickly. It is hard to look at yourself and get to your truth. But to my surprise what happened when I got real was my life started to transform and I felt a new peace within. By year three, I knew I had to share what I learned with the world. Jim could see changes in me, some he didn't always like. I was asserting myself because I had finally found my inner strength, but he gently encouraged me to become a healer, of course reminding me of the financial commitment we had made with my training.

"Peg, we've invested a lot in you, so you need to become a healer," Jim told me.

That led to my seeking out a part-time space, and now, here I am seven years later, with a flourishing full-time practice.

I'm not sure I would have believed it myself had you told me this is where I was going to end up about ten years ago. And now, because of all the inner work I have done to get to this point, I know I can help Jim and our whole family heal in the deepest ways imaginable.

Now that the shock of Jim's collapse is a few days behind us, and Makenzie's text last night reminded me of my training as an Energy Healer, I know what I need to do to help him. But first, I have to take care of myself.

Mid-morning at the hospital, we do a shift change: Jodie and I go home after my parents drop off Bunnie, Carlos, and Cookie at the hospital. I shower and hold a hot compress over a sty that has developed on my right eyelid over the last two days. I call my naturopath and explain what is happening. "Can you just call in a prescription ointment?"

"Of course," she says. I have quickly found that everyone is so accommodating in a crisis. Thank God for these continued acts of kindness! I text my friend and neighbor, Stephani, to see if she can send an email to all of my clients. I want to cancel appointments through January 2nd. I know it seems far off, but I need time for my entire family to heal.

At this moment, I don't trust myself with computers or anything that requires some brain cells, so Stephani is happy to oblige. She gets my clients organized into a group email and goes over my calendar to make sure we don't miss anyone who is scheduled. I am still not the best at asking for help, but I've improved rapidly in that department these last two days. When you are brought to the brink and have no choice, it becomes a lot easier to swallow your pride. As soon as she sends that email, I feel like a giant burden has been lifted from my shoulders.

At this point, I have slowly built my practice from part time to full time, five days a week, seeing four clients a day. I love what I do: guiding people to find their higher selves and to heal their physical, emotional, and spiritual aches and pains. Everyone has a different story to tell, or burden to lay down and heal. I see cult and incest survivors, women and men who have been physically or sexually abused, people with autoimmune diseases or cancer, children who have nightmares, or just everyday people who want to live a deeper, richer life but don't have the tools or courage to do it. With everyone I see, a piece of me heals, as well. There is always more to examine, look at, and move forward from.

As much as I love my clients, I know I have made the right choice. I don't see how I can go back to my practice if I have nothing left of myself to give. That, and given how close Jim came to dying, he needs all of me to help him recover and heal.

Stephani helps me pick up my prescription for my eye and runs me back up to the hospital around 12:30 p.m.

I walk in to find Jim with Dr. Abernathy, who is suggesting that he take the cough syrup with the pain meds together at night so he might be able to sleep. Someone comes in from radiology to do a chest X-ray. I text Bunnie the results: "Chest X-ray showed no new clots. All cardiac tests were normal. Blood work stable. Urine still very bloody, which she hopes will improve in the next day or two."

Jim is making slow, steady progress. His body has been through so much, but I feel like he has already made the choice to stay on Earth. We've come too far for him to die now, but there is also a part of me that knows I need to relinquish control over the situation...because, in the end, I don't have any. In my healing school, Alima always told us, "You're not in charge of anything. Your life is scripted by something larger than yourself. Call it God, spirit, the universe, whatever your faith wants to name that higher power. Just know that it's there, and it's calling the shots."

For me, it's divine knowing...my spidey sense that gets triggered during my healing sessions. When I allow myself to be a conduit for Earth energy, messages from the divine come through effortlessly. Not just in healing sessions, but also, from my experience, in the moments when life hangs in the balance.

Earlier today when I checked in on Jim's field, Spirit gave me two clear messages:

1. Jim is choosing to live.
2. Jim wouldn't have come back if living meant having brain damage.

It is going to be either 100% Jim or no Jim at all.

This divine knowing trumps everything. My husband is going to live, and with all of his faculties intact.

It might sound ludicrous, but you don't question it when God talks to you. You just have faith. It's like an intricate web; if I didn't have faith in God, I wouldn't receive these divine messages, but once I receive them, I don't dare question them, or that would break that web of faith and trust. My human self is terrified, but my spiritual self is at ease. This is the duality that shows up constantly in healing. If we were just spiritual creatures, life would be simple, but human aspects like our egos make us question and challenge the hell out of the spiritual guidance we receive.

At this point in Jim's recovery, the doctors turn their focus on his heart and clearing the blood clots out of his system. The discussion hasn't yet been broached about examining how well his brain is functioning, but I know it will come later.

I grab Jim's hand, and say "Honey, you're going to be OK." He smiles, but I'm not sure that he believes that. He doesn't buy into what he calls my "magical thinking."

One of the hardest things for me is that Jim doesn't tap into this same sense of divine knowing that I do. While I embarked on a spiritual journey when I started healing school, he did not. I believe we all have a different and unique journey with spirit or God in our lifetimes; Jim has faith but also relies on his brain and logic way more than I do. Although I'm a grounded person and Jim is the one who is constantly concocting new ideas and projects, we go about these matters in totally different ways. I fly by the seat of my pants and trust that all will be taken care of. I "navigate by starlight," as I like to call it. Jim usually thinks I'm nuts and need to get my head out of the clouds, but he's also learned to step aside when my intuition kicks in.

In this moment, I can sense that he is still experiencing massive anxiety and fear. I learned in healing school that if you break it down, there are just two types of energetic vibrations that exist in the world: love and fear. Love is the highest vibration, and fear is the lowest. You cannot give in to fear; you have to surrender to the *what is*. I will continue to hold Jim in love to transmute his fear, and help him heal energetically.

Six: Integration

I start energy work on Jim that afternoon. My first challenge is putting his auric field back together, and the second is bringing in higher vibrational energy to transform the fear. My working conditions stink. In a typical healing session, I first prepare myself, and then my space, for my client. My healing space is like a womb: There are no windows, and I have soft drapes floating on the ceiling that feel like clouds. The entire space is extremely quiet.

In contrast, the hospital is bright, loud, and full of beeping machines. It is also full of constant interruptions by doctors, nurses, or people wanting to take blood from Jim.

All the same, I try not to let myself be distracted. As a hands-on healer, I pull Earth energy up through my feet, into my hands, and then directly into the client. The first step in a session is asking the client's permission. I have worked on Jim in my office and he has signed a waiver, so I take that as a green light to start working on him now, since technically, he is a current client of mine.

I also remind myself that my attachments can play no part in any of this. I can't insert my own intentions for what Jim's healing should look like. He calls the shots and lays down the plan of how he wants to heal. When I am healing, I connect to the client's inner healer, or inner physician. Dr. John Upledger wrote a book called *Your Inner Physician and You* that explains the concept that we are born with this inner wisdom about how to heal ourselves, most of us just haven't been taught how to access this deep well of knowledge. What I have seen in my healing work is that "your issues are in your tissues." Everything we need to know is showing up in our bodies, mentally, or on a spiritual level.

This means that Jim is essentially in charge of healing himself, and I want him to be. After all, the point of healing work is to teach my people how to heal themselves. I always tell my clients, "My goal isn't to have you come in and see me forever." I give them their wings, and then they go fly.

Given the situation I am in, I know that I need to modify my healing techniques. Jim's body has been through too much, and his system won't tolerate a typical one-hour session. Part of being an energy healer is controlling the flow. You are an open conduit, but you can push, pull, or stop earth energy. When you start a healing, you pick up cues from a person's auric field and chakras (the spinning energy centers of the body), as well as how much energy they can let flow through their system. As a rule of thumb, children need less, because their auric fields are smaller and they usually have experienced less trauma. Not to mention, they are more open. When stress and traumatic situations like car wrecks or serious injuries occur, we layer up to protect ourselves. I compare energy healing to pulling back the layers of an onion. You are slowly working your way to the middle, which, in healing terms, is your core star. This is your Divine spark, the light that resides in all of us.

I start by working for one or two minutes at a time, finding quiet moments between the beeps and interruptions. Jim alternates between coughing, trying to sleep, and having more blood drawn from him.

Jim reminds me of a child because of his fractured auric field, this makes him appear vulnerable and small. The first thing I encounter when I get hands on is that it's hard to connect with the lower layers of his field. His flow is jerky and disjointed. I can see that having your heart stop three times and then restart really messes with your energy field. I start small, bringing the pieces of his aura in closer to his physical body. I can tell that I need to slowly reintroduce Jim's field to his physical body.

In healing school, we call this allowing, or integration. I connect to Jim's inner healer through the layers of his auric field. Each layer has its own unique qualities and properties, with color, density, and textures. When I was trained, we spent a few months on each layer of the field and the corresponding chakra. We would learn about its complexities, what color the layer/chakra is, and what that represents on a spiritual level. We also learned about how the body is affected by distortions in each layer and chakra. I still read books and take classes on the subject. I don't think that anyone can ever know everything there is to know about our energy field and chakra system. Doing this work is like going on a magic carpet ride every day.

I try to maintain my sense of humor, which helps keep me in a state of balance and neutrality. Not an easy feat, considering Jim's layers are a hot mess. You want a system to look even, with equal spacing between the layers and a solid flow of energy. Think of a smooth ocean wave: The tide flows in and then it flows out. I have worked on one other person who had a near-death experience, and Jim's field looks like his. Disjointed, not connected. In some spots, the field is flat and all stuck together, or crushed. I wonder if the feeling of that last breath leaving your body is what makes everything collapse. It appears that losing oxygen is similar to a crushing sensation. If your physical body is no longer occupied, then maybe the field layers feel like they don't need to protect the body anymore? It's my best guess at this point.

I switch tactics and ask Spirit to hold Jim up to his highest good. Then I run pure change to holding light. If we break energy down, what is it, really? Light, sound, and vibration. The use of colors is important in healing, with each color representing different things. For now, I fall back to the easiest one, pure white light, hold Jim up to his highest good.

Another part of energy work is holding sacred space for someone so they can heal. This is like setting the stage for a scene in a play. What would Jim need to get him through this? I know that I need to hold him gently in white light and be an open, clear channel of energy for him to access as needed. Being a healer is a dance, because in one respect you are in control and can make changes in the field; on the other hand, you are just a conduit and allow the energy to flow where it needs to go, and then you follow it. Then, there are times when you just hand it over to higher guidance, like spirit guides, ascended masters, or angels, and allow them to work through you. When you are working with the Divine, you don't always know what is healing when—it's all part of the mystery.

I continue to do little pieces of energy work throughout the afternoon on Jim, and then Landon, Logan, and Madison arrive to check in on their dad and to bring him the cheese pizza he requested. In the order of things Jim loves, pizza is number four on the list. God, family, and chips take the top three spots. I take this as a good sign, especially as I see the kids relax, take a breath, and just like their mom, surrender to their new reality. Landon wiggles in to hold his dad's hand, which, although swollen and bruised, is the least painful part of his body at this point.

"Is it OK if I hold your hand like this, Dad?" Landon whispers.

Jim smiles. "Yes, I love you, buddy."

I take a photo of their hands to capture that raw, sweet moment. I can feel my heart let out a sigh.

The kids notice that while my stress level is off the charts, for the first time in a long time, their dad is relaxed enough to drop his type A personality. He is softer and more open and accessible. Before, he would have an agenda and a plan to start every day. I think this is why Jim and I are so good together. I can run a tight ship if I have to, but it's not my first choice. To be honest, the kids probably need a little more discipline and structure from me, and more softness and affection from Jim.

I can sense that Jim is living in the present moment, and all agendas and plans died along with him on our hallway rug. He knows he is no longer in charge—of anything. The miracle of being alive when you should be dead has changed the entire game.

The days are easy to navigate, but as soon as the kids leave for home, the sweet exchange between father and children crashes to the floor and reality sets in. Night falls, it gets dark, and Jim is scared to sleep.

"I want the lights on," he says. "Also, I need a fan that's circulating air, and the hospital door has to be kept open." The last moment he had experienced on the Earth plane was everything fading to black. I know that when night falls, it triggers that feeling Jim had of slowly losing oxygen, and it kicks up a massive claustrophobic reaction. Jim fears he won't wake up and feels like he is in a coffin when he sleeps.

I spend the night watching the hands of the hospital clock spin in circles backwards to reset itself for daylight saving time. I continue to do bits and pieces of energy work. Jim still feels stuck somewhere within the layers of his field, but I am not able to track the pieces to figure out where they are. I continue to keep myself open as a conduit of Earth energy, so that his inner healer can access the white light through me. I hold his hand and run energy to boost his inner strength.

Come on, Jim. Please find the pieces of yourself that got scattered and bring them back.

The energy system and physical body work in a magical synchronicity and flow. I'm worried that if he can't pull his auric field back together on the fifth layer, then maybe the Divine plan is saying it's time for him to leave the Earth plane. However, Jim is holding his own on the physical plane...but barely. Logan says he looks like a beat-up drug addict, which isn't far from the truth. His arms are now bright purple, he's lost weight and his eyes are a little sunken, and he is still peeing blood. Worst of all, his hematocrit level is still slowly dropping.

I am doing all that I know how to do as a healer, but not knowing what the Divine plan has in store for my husband makes surrender a challenge. This may be the hardest part of healing, especially when you are working with a loved one. Staying neutral and having no agenda is next to impossible. I will have to navigate carefully to allow the Divine to work through me and guide Jim through the immense healing his mind, body, and spirit will undertake in the next days, weeks, and probably months.

What Jim has experienced is what I would refer to as a complete healing crisis. When something like this occurs, you never go back to status quo. I suspect this will be true for Jim.

My mantra since Jim's collapse has been: "Love will get me through this." Today, I add a few words: "... if I surrender, allow, breathe."

Seven: Broken

I was lulled into a false sense of peace last night, still clinging to the image of Landon holding Jim's hand. I feel comfortable enough to go home and shower, grab new clothes, and come back up. I leave Jodie with Jim, and my friend Maureen picks me up at 8 a.m. at the hospital with a chai tea. Simple comforts matter. It's nice to talk with a girlfriend and download all that has happened in the last four days. (That's an eternity given what Jim has gone through thus far.) As I start to speak, I realize how fragile I have become.

"I don't know if I can continue on this rollercoaster," I tell her as I settle into her passenger seat. "This is all too much. I'm so tired." I start to cry, of course, since I cry constantly now. I laugh inside thinking that my healing school teacher Alima would be happy that I am finally "congruent." Meaning my emotions are matching what is happening in the present moment.

"Peg, you are one of the strongest people I know, and you can handle anything," Maureen says.

I sigh. "I don't feel strong at all. I'm so worried about losing Jim, and my kids not having a father!" That's the cloud constantly looming over me.

"I'm working on finding you and Logan a therapist," Maureen says, squeezing my hand. "I'm so sorry you both witnessed his collapse. God, that couldn't have been easy!"

"I just question why I didn't see it coming," I say. "I should have sensed he was in trouble." I close my eyes, and feel a sense of guilt wash over me.

"You did, Peg!" she exclaims. "You didn't go to work...something told you to turn around and go home to take him to the emergency room! Just imagine what could've happened if you weren't there!"

"That's true, I guess," I agree with her, drying my tears.

I give her a hug when she pulls up to my house. "I love you so much! Thank you for everything, and for distracting Landon with play dates. He needs a second mom."

She squeezes me tightly. "Look, Peg, you've been through an immense trauma. This is your husband. You're so close to him, and it makes it harder to see what's coming. You are a talented healer who has great intuition—don't forget that. Jim *needs* you to help him heal."

I wave goodbye and head into the house. I get more fuel from the round of hugs I receive from my kids. I let

Carlos, Cookie, and Bunnie know that I am going to shower and then head back up to the hospital. At 10 a.m., we all go back there together. Maureen's kind words and hugs from my kids have boosted my spirits. I feel ready for the day ahead.

Logan had driven his own car up so he could say hello to his Dad and then bring Jodie home to sleep. Shortly after they leave, a urologist shows up. His demeanor when he walks in reminds me of the evil queen in *Snow White*: cold, unfeeling, and mean. As soon as he starts talking, he confirms this. He tells us matter-of-factly, "Jim is internally bleeding, and we aren't sure from where. If the bleeding doesn't stop, he will slowly bleed to death, but if I do exploratory surgery, he will most likely bleed to death, as well."

THUD.

You can feel everyone's optimism and perseverance slip away with this news. The evil queen has just shattered my hopes into a thousand pieces. After all the hurdles he has jumped over thus far, Jim's life is still hanging in the balance.

Jim and I shoot looks back and forth. I can feel his fear rising and am trying to hold mine in check, as I say,

"Well, then give us a couple days to pray the bleeding stops. Surgery is not an option if you know it will kill him."

"Fine," the urologist replies emotionlessly. "I'll give you 24 hours, but I'm warning you, if the bleeding doesn't stop, I will have to proceed with surgery." As quickly as he swooped in, he leaves the room.

"It's going to be OK," I reassure Jim.

"It *has* to be," he says, his voice rising in panic. "I've survived three cardiac arrests. I find it hard to believe that at this stage in the game, I'm going to slowly bleed to death!"

"I agree. I need to take a minute..." I tell him.

Trying to combat the hopelessness, I retreat to the corner of his room in the silver tower and break down. Bunnie just holds my hand and lets me sob quietly. I don't want Jim to hear, or see, me crack.

I am broken.

I feel my jolt of confidence from the early morning melt away. Frankly, I'm also angry at the urologist and his poor bedside manner. Way to break that kind of news.

I whisper to Bunnie, "Now I know why the hospital windows don't open...I might just jump."

I text Mike shortly after to share the news: "Jim's hematocrit levels are dropping, might need a blood transfusion, internal bleeding from somewhere but not sure where."

Typical Mike. His text back cracks me up: "I've done direct lines before so if you want me to hook up and provide O+ lemme know." Spoken like a true EMT. In the moments of the lowest lows, it feels like I'm getting little shots in the arm of encouragement and support.

Carlos, Cookie, Bunnie, Jim, and I are still processing the urologist's news, and none of us know what to do or say. After my breakdown in the corner, I feel defeated. Jim is visibly upset, as well, so I focus my attention back on him. "Honey, we have to focus on one thing at a time. You have come so far, and now we just need to pray and ask other people to pray the bleeding stops," I try and reassure him.

"I know, but I'm tired," he responds with a sigh. "My body has been through too much...they don't even know where the bleeding is coming from." My heart drops as I realize that my husband is beginning to give up hope.

At some point last night, a tech came in and did an ultrasound of Jim's bladder and kidneys. From that ultrasound, they were not able to pinpoint any places where Jim is internally bleeding. At the same time, she did an ultrasound of both of Jim's legs to check on the size of the

DVT in his left leg. They had done an initial scan when Jim was in the CCU, but this gave us a closer look at the size of the DVT so we could determine whether or not it's shrinking. Finally, we have a reference point to look at that is vaguely comforting...because maybe now we can make sure it's actually going away.

"I'm going to send out a request for prayers and focused intention for the bleeding to stop on Caring Bridge," I tell Jim. "We have a lot of people pulling for our family and praying for you, so I just know you are going to make it through this hurdle."

Caring Bridge has been a great tool to get information out to our community, friends, and loved ones. Wendy, my friend of 30 years, has been coming to the hospital daily, and was able to create a Jim Rodrigues web page that detailed what happened on November 2nd. I've been feeding her updates to post or asking her to write one for me as the days progress. This way, there is just one source of information that everyone in our lives can refer to, and anyone can read the updates at any time if they follow Jim's story.

Jim and I both believe in the power of prayer, and that there is a God or higher power. We were both raised Catholic, and our similar faith backgrounds have made a difference in our marriage, especially in instances like this one, and Logan getting diagnosed with NF1. Some might see the healing school concepts and teachings as directly conflicting with the tenets of Catholicism, but for me becoming a healer just made this intangible world of faith more real for me. In school we learned about the power of prayer and the collective, and how focused intention can make manifest.

I breathe deeply and let my anger melt into fuel, wiping away my tears and digging up some more courage from deep within. I know that anger is a lower energetic vibration that is not going to help Jim in any way at this moment.

I harness my inner warrior spirit and go to work. Part of healing school was faking it until you make it. I don't know how you energetically stop bleeding, but I will sure as hell try. There is a saying in healing school: "Imagination is the gateway to spirit." I may not know what to do in every single situation, but I rely on my imagination, training, and instructions from spirit.

What I like about my work is I can be running energy and no one really knows from the outside what's happening because it looks like you are doing nothing. How you run energy is start visualizing that you are, and before you know it you start sensing the pulses of energy coming from the earth and into your system. When I started running energy in school it was zings and zaps, now with practice and intention I can feel a steady stream of energy coming up through my body and into my hands.

In this environment I have to seize every opportunity I can to heal Jim. I put my hands on his feet and check in on his field, and I realize that the fractured pieces of his aura are floating in and reattaching. It's like I'm watching pieces of a puzzle that someone threw in the air, starting to fit together again to reconnect the picture.

Energy healing is the ultimate multitasking, I'm pulling energy up through me, then transferring it to Jim. Through training I "see" what is happening through my third eye (clarasentient) and also listen to what spirit is saying (claraaudient). Based on the conversation with spirit happening in my head, I tweak things here and there.

As Jim's aura works to rebuild itself, I am sending healing white light to his liver and kidneys at the same time. His heart feels too delicate to work on at this stage, as it's still in a state of shock from the cardiac arrests. Sometimes, when running Earth energy is too strong for a system, I switch to reverse Reiki. In school we learned that Reiki means tapping into universal energy, or that Reiki is more free flowing than Earth Energy, which can be directed or controlled. When you do reverse Reiki, you are pulling out stagnant energy from a person's system instead of allowing energy to flow in. I have been doing this on Jim's lungs to work the clots out, and on his ribs to release physical pain. Jim is unaware of how much energy work I am doing, but I know him well enough to recognize that he would appreciate my efforts.

When I turn myself over as an instrument for the Divine to work through, I feel like I am guided and I am no longer using my brain. I am in a different dimension when I work. The layers of your field coordinate with dimensions of existence. Each layer also coordinates with the chakra of the same number, so the first layer of the field ties into your first chakra, which is connected to rootedness and security. This first layer is close to the body. Layers one through three represent our connection to Earth, our life force, and our will. When you shift to the fourth layer of the field, or fourth dimension, you are moving into the spiritual realms, or what most people refer to as the astral plane. I have found freedom working in the astral, instead of being in your head, there is a gentle flow and hum to this layer of the field that you just sink into. It is from this place of no attachment that I receive messages and instructions.

As I check in on the first three of Jim's layers now, I can see the pieces of the auric field coming in, but can also see that he has been so fractured that coming back into these lower layers will be a huge challenge. I am having a difficult time sensing and seeing Jim's first through third chakras, but I can clearly see his fourth. This tells me that Jim still hasn't connected with the Earth plane completely, which makes me believe that he could still make a choice to live or die. That door hasn't closed yet for him, he could still decide to leave.

When you die, your chakras shut down, starting with the first chakra, then the second and third and so on, until you ascend out of your body through your seventh, or crown, chakra. I frown to myself, Jim is what I would call an extreme case. I am using all of my skills but at this juncture, I'm not sure what has happened to Jim's lower layers and chakras, but they all seem gelled together as I look deeper. So, on one side of the coin, he fractured his aura into pieces, which is clearly a side effect of the cardiac arrest; on the other side, it also looks like he pulled deeply into himself to survive, which is probably what resulted in his first three energy layers gelling together. I call it "energetic puckering," like sucking yourself into a straw to disappear. I am determined to find out what happened to create this, but for now, I just hold sacred space for him to heal and specifically hold intention for the internal bleeding to stop. When you hold sacred space for someone you are connecting to Spirit and asking for them to be held in light and prayer for their highest good.

People often ask me if I'm a psychic. I wouldn't classify myself that way, per se; I once told a client that I'm more of an instrument for spirit to work through. I know that everyone's energy field has a story to tell, and it doesn't lie. I'm a kinesthetic healer, meaning once I get hands on I can see and read the field, but it's not like I'm walking down the street reading the energy fields of everyone I pass by.

As traumas and dramas happen to us, they leave a trail of imprints on your energy field. I decipher these so that I can clear and shift these imprints. The energy field supports your physical body, and acts as a layer of protection around you. As I clear and change the field, most clients notice that they feel stronger or their physical pain goes away. Lots of spiritual teachers talk about the "pain body," and there are many schools of thought about what pain is, or what it represents. Usually, pain is the result of an emotional block, an injury, or a person's belief systems. I believe in what Dr. Bruce Lipton explains in his book

Biology of Belief: that we have the power to change our DNA on a cellular level.

Basically, if everyone is telling you that you are in pain, or that you're sick and going to die, you don't have to believe it. Your thoughts can change your destiny. On the flip side of that though, is the fact that maybe your destiny is to die at a young age, or get cancer. The hardest one for me to sort out with the Divine is young children that get sick. But I don't think there is anything wrong with believing you can change at any moment. It takes faith and courage.

I also feel that everyone has the capacity to heal themselves, and that anything is possible. After all, that's why I'm still here, hanging on to every sliver of information I'm receiving about Jim's energetic state.

I shake off my wandering thoughts and keep holding an intention for the internal bleeding to stop. Like prayer, I believe strongly in the power of setting clear intentions, sending light into dark places, and holding everyone up to their highest potential to heal. I am still holding Jim's feet when I am interrupted by a phlebotomist wanting to take more blood from my husband.

Jesus, vampires, all of you! Go away!

I grudgingly step away from Jim to check my phone. I see a text that makes me smile. I guess prayers *do* work. I read a message from Blake, our old nanny that we all love dearly.

"Hey Peg! I moved back and I wanted to come say hi to the kids! Miss you guys!"

Blake is Maureen's neighbor. She went to college in Arizona years ago, so I'm surprised that she is popping back into our lives at the exact moment we need her.

I say a silent thank you and text her back: "I need to hire you for help. Call Maureen and get the story." Even though Carlos and Cookie have agreed to stay through Thanksgiving, I want their energy to be spent focused on Jim and his healing. Plus, they don't drive, and I don't want to stretch my parents too thin, either, by asking them to drive my kids all over town.

Blake can sense something is wrong and texts back: "Is everything OK?? I will call Maureen. Let me know if there's anything I can do. I'd love to help."

"No, not OK," I reply. My emotions are all over the map today. I am having a hard time staying grounded and being here for Jim. I have stuffed so much down inside myself in the last four days, and the evil queen's poor bedside manner this morning has triggered a cascade of feelings: sadness, fear, frustration, exhaustion, despair, happiness, gratitude...and it's all coming out over the course of the day.

Peg, get it together—you are stronger than you know. Jim needs you to be clear today so you can hold sacred space for him to heal and allow your energy to support him to give him strength.

I start saying my mantra in my head to help me re-ground. "Love will get me through this if I surrender, allow, breathe."

As I focus on my breathing, a basket mysteriously shows up full of good things to eat—fresh blueberries, kombucha, and my favorite, chocolate! I see that it is from Holly, my hairdresser. I text her immediately: "Are you here at the hospital? I need a break."

She replies: "I can come right back, turning around."

I keep breathing and focus on grounding and releasing my emotions as I walk down to the parking lot to get some fresh air.

"In the parking lot breathing," I text back.

She shows up around 3:45 p.m. and gives me a giant hug. Of course, despite all the damage control, I start to cry, so we go sit in my car. I give her the summary of the day, screaming and yelling between sobs: "This is all too much! I am a good human! For God's sake, I heal people for a living! I don't deserve this!"

Obviously, I know that bad things can happen to good people and that none of us are immune to the twists and turns of the universe...but for the time being, I need to vent. In my healing school, we called this wallowing in our lower self. I typically refer to it as having a shit fit. I'm usually a little more calm and collected, especially with friends who don't know me all that well. Holly has never seen me like this; usually, I am reading magazines in her chair with tinfoil on my head. My communication with most of the world at this point has been through Caring Bridge, so I can tell she wasn't prepared for my unleashing. Still, she takes it in stride. She just allows me to let it all go and then gives me another big hug.

I wipe my tears and tell her, "I have to go back up. I'm sure Jim is missing me by now."

I feel better for a couple of hours before my energy begins to dip. Although my healing training helped me develop greater self-care and awareness of what is happening in my body at any given moment, I feel myself reverting to the "old Peg." The one who found it easy to melt into a puddle of defeat, overwhelmed and feeling hopeless. I send out another silent prayer to the Divine mystery at the center of all of this. I am going to need all the help I can get.

By dinnertime, we are all exhausted. At some point in the day, Jodie joined us after taking a nap, and is now leaving to go home with Carlos and Cookie.

"The pop-out recliner here isn't working for me," she says, rubbing her eyes, clearly exhausted. "Is it OK if Bunnie takes the night shift tonight?"

I nod. "Absolutely." I give her a big hug, sensing that she's probably as sore and wiped out as I am. She's leaving tomorrow night, and I know she needs some rest. We all do.

I check my phone at 6:15 p.m. and find a text from my friend Wendy: "How's Jim? Worried."

I had been radio silent for the entire day, and because she is one of those deeply connected friends, she could sense there was something wrong and had texted me at 4 p.m.

I feel bad for ignoring her first text and respond: "Bad day. I'll call soon."

By now, my anger from earlier is completely gone and I feel stuck in a well of deep fear and sadness.

Jim has to live.

I stir myself into a frenzy again, thinking of the life we have shared. A flurry of random moments washes over me: our random meeting in a bar; our fast and romantic courtship; all the flowers he sent as an expression of his love for me; our wedding day; buying our first home; our first dog, Boston, a Labrador/Dalmatian mix (God, Jim loved that dog so much); the births of each of our four children; our ability as a couple to laugh our heads off whenever we needed comic relief.

My husband deserves to celebrate our next milestones. Madison is leaving for college next fall. After all our hard work as parents, we are just getting to the *fun* phase: launching our kids out of the nest. Makenzie has a lot more soccer to play, and what about all of them getting married and having their own children? And Landon...once more, I can't bear the thought of him losing his dad at age 11.

I excuse myself and retreat to a little waiting room near the elevators on the eighth floor. I call Wendy and immediately break down: "Jim is still internally bleeding! If it doesn't stop, he could die. The urologist came in this morning and said either he'll bleed to death slowly, or if he does surgery, he could bleed to death from the surgery."

Wendy's voice is steady and unwavering. "Jim is *strong,* Peg—he will pull through! I'll write a Caring Bridge post for you that explains what's going on and ask for more prayers."

"Anything will help. I have to stay firm in my belief that there is a higher power at work here. Jim wouldn't have survived that first day only to die now," I tell her, reassuring myself more than anything else.

A nurse walks by as I am crying, pacing, and cursing into the phone. She gives me a look of concern and pauses to mouth, "Are you OK?"

I nod and try to smile. While I'm not about holding my emotions back, I need to stay in the highest vibration possible. I am no good to Jim when I'm broken down and defeated.

I have allowed the negative energy and opinion of one doctor to shape my entire day....great!

When I hang up with Wendy, I trust that her support will carry me through to the morning. Reading her Caring Bridge post a few hours later, as well as all the enthusiastic responses, I breathe deeply and smile.

Journal entry by Wendy Thomas—11/6/2016—Jim had a good night, only to be followed by a tough day. There is still blood in his urine. Ultrasound of his bladder and kidneys are good so they aren't sure where the internal bleeding is coming from. They've been titrating his heparin (blood thinner med) to figure out what dose is best. Doing surgery was discussed as an option but because of the blood thinners, there is a fear that he might not pull through. This evening the amount of blood in his urine seems to be lessening. Right now the family asks for lots of prayers...especially praying for the internal bleeding to stop over the next couple days. It was looking like Jim would be able to go home Wednesday, but the most recent development, given all that his body has been through, is that he'll need to be in a rehab facility to heal and gain strength before he goes home. Peg and the family very much appreciate your continued love, support, and prayers.

I imagine myself taking in all the prayers of my community. It reassures me that we are connected, and that loving each other is the most important thing we can do. I have always been able to see the Divine plan and the threads that link us together, but the last four days have driven this home. Otherwise, I wouldn't be able to explain the little moments of synchronicity: my intuition telling me to TURN AROUND and head back home the morning of November 2nd, my brother coming out of the woods and answering my call at just the right moment, my old nanny texting me out of the blue that she is home and available, all the little gestures of kindness from strangers.

I feel comforted and uplifted at the end of this tumultuous day. I can feel myself coming down from the activities of the past 24 hours.

Jim and I manage to end the night with me gently running energy into his system and nudging pieces of his field back into place. I make a mental note that Jim's body and energy system are completely out of sync and rhythm. I need more of his auric field back before I can address the flow of the field. After all, you need to have a field before you can do something with it.

Jim still isn't connecting to Earth energy through his foot chakras, or what I call grounding. Given that he almost died, this connection appears to be temporarily disrupted. That, and on the physical plane, he still finds it terribly difficult to move from bed to chair. I'm hoping that he will be ready to reconnect to the Earth plane soon.

You have to come back, Jim...keep fighting.

A nurse named Bella brings in a funny-looking device called a spirometer. She wants Jim to start using it right away. The device measures his lung capacity and encourages his lungs to heal. You have to take in a long slow intake of air, and when Jim takes in his first breath, he whispers, "This is what it must be like to take a bong hit."

I collapse into a fit of giggles. "You've never smoked pot a day in your life, honey."

If Jim were to die, these are the little moments that I would miss the most. Jim is so damn funny, and his comedic timing is perfect. Who else could make me laugh till my sides hurt, even when I'm in the midst of the biggest despair I've ever known?

He gives me a weird look and laughs. "I know."

Throughout the night, I hold Jim in the highest vibration possible: the seventh layer, which is brilliant white and gold light. It's all I can do at the moment. I still haven't figured out how to stop the bleeding energetically, since it's become clear to me over the day that there are various ways the body can respond to complications. It's like a chain reaction of different things that makes it hard to know what to focus on to heal first.

I remind myself: *It's not your job to fix Jim. All you can do is pray and hold him up to his highest good. This is his journey, and you are just a sacred witness.*

Bunnie nudges me out of my spot in the recliner chair next to Jim in the wee hours of the morning.

"Peg, you need to get a couple hours of sleep, so move to the bench where you can lay flat." I am starting to curse the recliner chair, just like Jodie did. It's so uncomfortable, but Jim likes me there because I am right next to him, while the bench is across the room.

I see Jim is sleeping, and I gladly switch spots. I say my prayers like I did as a little girl. "Please God, let my husband live. I need him, our children need him, and he's too young to go now. Amen."

I am hoping to wake up and realize all my prayers have been answered.

Eight: Faith

The first of my prayers to be answered is getting some sleep, although I only get a couple hours at most. Jim has Bunnie wake me up around 4 a.m. so he can pee. We have a routine down now. I put on rubber gloves and grab the pee bottle, and Jim does his thing. I leave it in the bathroom to be measured and examined by the nurse on duty, take my gloves off, wash my hands, and then give Jim the hand sanitizer to wash his hands.

This time, when I look at his urine, it seems like the heavy, thick "Merlot pee" is now a lighter shade of red.

"Jim, it looks more like red Kool-aid this morning," I exclaim happily. "I think the bleeding is slowing down."

"I sure hope you're right, honey," Jim whispers in that sexy low voice. I am starting to wonder if his throat or vocal cords are permanently damaged from the ventilator.

We have officially reached Day 6 in the hospital. I can't believe what has happened to our lives and that I am happy about Kool-aid colored pee. Jim is progressing slowly. He has moved from the bed to the chair, which is a colossal effort, but he does not have the strength to be up and walking about. He is still on oxygen because his lungs are still compromised by the clots, his arms are a nice shade of purple and black, his neck is still tinged with orange from the IVC surgery, and now he has a liquid bandage that is curling and starting to roll up on his neck. It resembles a piece of peeling skin. I shudder just looking at it.

He is finally able to go to sleep at night without thinking he won't wake up, but every night, as darkness falls, he insists on keeping the hospital room door open.

Although I've been with Jim throughout the entire ordeal, I find it hard to believe this is my husband, who was so young and vital just two weeks ago, because he looks so beat up, bruised, and exhausted.

I trade spots with Bunnie, giving her the bench so we can all get some more sleep, and settle into the dreaded recliner. My body hurts, especially my knees. I have gotten used to the fact that standing on these concrete floors 24/7 is probably going to cause me permanent damage. Also, the rest of my body, my back, and neck need a serious chiropractic adjustment. Jim and I are quite a pair, and although we are like a couple of broken-down wagons with the wheels coming off, I give a silent thank-you that we *are* still a pair.

After a couple hours of trying to sleep in the horrible recliner and listening to Jim cough, I give up and text my brother Mike at 6:11 a.m. He will be flying home to Montana today and I want to see him before he goes. "I am at hospital until 10:30–10:45 a.m. You were a champ helping me these past six days. Love you!"

He texts back, "OK, let me fire up work and I will update you what time I will stop by Evergreen on my way to the airport."

I reply, "Dodged a bullet, urologist said. Considering where we came from, Kool-aid colored urine is great."

He quickly responds, "Oh good! We are on our way up."

The evil queen urologist had come by early in the morning and was able to look at Jim's Kool-aid pee. (I know I won't ever be able to drink it or Merlot ever again.)

"It looks like the bleeding is slowing down," he'd said, agreeing with my assessment earlier that morning. "I think at this point we do NOT need to do surgery. I am happy to let you have another day or two to allow the bleeding to stop since it's trending in the right direction."

He had left as quickly as he'd come, while Bunnie, Jim, and I all sat there for a minute, stunned and happy, allowing his words to sink in.

"You're healing, honey—you are going to pull through," I had told Jim.

I teared up, and for the first time in six days, I trusted 100% that my husband is going to live. Prayer number two answered!

Usually, my childhood prayers were simple: "Watch over me and my family as I sleep." Last night, I asked God to stop the bleeding and let my husband live. It looks like he listened.

Thinking about it all, I let out a deep sigh and feel a momentary peace flood my system. All of yesterday's emotions and fears fade away.

Shortly after, my brother and parents come by to check on Jim.

"Mike, thank you for everything," Jim whispers. "It meant so much that you flew out the instant I collapsed."

"You bet," my brother says. "Keep fighting, because you've come a long way in six days." He turns to me and squeezes my hand. "And please text any time you need me. I love you, sis!" My sister, Sara, flew home yesterday, so she can take over as sibling support for me. I owe my brother big time for swooping in like an angel and taking care of me and my family.

I give him a big hug. My dad turns to Jim and gives him a hopeful smile. "You really are a fighter, so keep battling. We'll come by later," he says.

You never know what your parents think of the spouse you choose for yourself (especially since my dad is so low-key he doesn't say much about anything), but in that moment, I can truly see that he feels immense love for Jim. My dad is a strong, proud man who grew up on a farm and admires hard work. Jim had fought to live, and I know my dad's respect for my husband has just increased tenfold.

I give my parents a hug and wave goodbye to my family. I then take a moment to check in on Jim's energy field, grabbing his feet and watching as the energy flows up his legs. I sigh. He is still having a heck of a time grounding to Earth, but I can sense that the urologist's words about the bleeding slowing down have shifted something in Jim. His auric field is stronger, and for the first time, the pieces of his field have gelled back together, but only in the upper half of his body.

It's strange; energetically, Jim looks like he has been cut in half. A person's third chakra is located just below the sternum, and on Jim's body, there seems to be a line or barrier in this place. He's not able to pull energy all the way up from Earth into his upper chakras. I don't have time to figure out why, as I'm interrupted by a nurse taking Jim's morning vitals. But at least I've confirmed that some deep healing has occurred.

After the nurse leaves, Cookie, Carlos, and Jodie show up in Jim's room at 10:30 a.m. One thing about having four kids is that you have a big support network. One of our neighbors, Pam, got wind of what had happened to Jim and offered to help any way she could. Her middle son goes to the high school down the street from the hospital, so she picked up Cookie and Carlos and Jodie, then dropped them off on her way back from taking her son to school. We all hug. I have to admit that the mood is quite celebratory.

Cookie is ecstatic. "I'm so happy that the bleeding is stopping on its own!"

I go to Jim, squeeze his hand, and ask, "Do you have everything you need, honey? Don't forget there may be some therapists stopping by." They are looking at moving Jim to the Acute Rehab Unit, which requires some tests. "I'm taking Bunnie home now, and then I have to meet with Blake. I'm so glad she's back home for a bit...I'm hiring her to help us until you've fully recovered."

"I'm good," Jim gives me the go-ahead. "I'm so glad Blake is here for us. Tell her thank you for me."

121

I give him a kiss before leaving with Bunnie. I have given up all hope of running my house and children's schedules the way I usually do, so I wasn't joking when I texted Blake that I would hire her. She doesn't have a job in Seattle yet, so this is the perfect way for her to make money until she finds a real one.

Thank you, God, for all the prayer requests that have been answered in the last few hours and in the last six days. I feel held and loved by my family, friends, and our community.

After one more glance at Jim to make sure he's good, I go home to shower and plan on meeting Blake at 11:30 a.m.

Bunnie immediately heads upstairs to Makenzie's room, where she and Jodie have been sleeping, to go to bed; understandably, she is wiped out. As I shower, I try to imagine the hot water washing away all the fears and doubts I've had about Jim's survival. If the bleeding is slowing down, I have no doubt he will make it. I get out, dry off, and blow-dry my hair. I'm beginning to feel like myself again. Then, I hear the doorbell ring.

I run downstairs and fling the front door open. It's Blake. I feel a huge weight lift as I wrap her in a big hug and exclaim, "Blake, I am *so* happy you're here!"

Blake had called Maureen, who filled her in on the details of Jim's collapse. She clearly understands just how much I need help. We consider her part of our family, and I am touched by her concern for me as she asks, "Peg, are you OK? I can't believe this is happening to your family."

"No, I'm definitely not OK, but let's get through what I need from you before I break down," I reply, not ready to be swept away by another tide of emotion. We have logistics to sort out.

We move through the house as I talk about our daily routines and describe some of the systems I have in place to run a family of six: "I need you to be there for Landon and Makenzie. Kenz is in the middle of driver's ed and needs driving experience, which I don't even have the bandwidth for right now. Landon is the one I'm most concerned about, so just watch him and let me know if you notice a change in his behavior. This has been really hard on the kids, but I've sheltered them from the fact that they almost lost their Dad many times over the last six days. They are seeing Jim in stages as he slowly improves, and I'm just trying to keep their lives as normal as possible."

Luckily, she has already spent two summers as our nanny. At 22, she is mature, responsible, and has a good head on her shoulders. "Don't worry Peg, I'll figure it out with the kids via texting and just roll with the day-to-day events, OK?"

I run my life old school–style with a paper calendar, which I pass over to her.

"Here's my life in a nutshell," I tell her, smiling. "I'm passing the torch, and I'm giving you my password for the computer if you need to check my emails, or you can ask Kenz to hack it."

I walk her from room to room to reacquaint her with our house and what belongs where. That's when I see Jim's jacket, which was ripped off him by paramedics, on the ground underneath our piano. Blake hears my sharp intake of breath.

"Peg?" she asks, a note of concern in her voice. This time, the tears come and I don't even try to hold them back. It feels like there is no end to them. But I don't have time for tears, so I wipe them away after a few moments.

"I'll be OK, seriously," I say, and give her an extra house key and alarm fob, wrapping her in a big hug again. "I adore you, Blake. Thank you for helping me and my family. We really need you, probably for a month or more. I understand if you get a real job in the process, but I'll take you as long as you have the time to give," I tell her.

Blake gives me a sympathetic squeeze. "No problem, Peg. I'm so glad that I can help, and so happy I texted you to come by and say hello," she says. "Life has a funny way of making things work out, huh?"

I laugh and wipe away more tears. "I'm glad you think so, because this is going to be one hell of a ride. I need to get back up to the hospital to be with Jim, so when I'm home, I'm just here to shower, grab clothes, and go back up. I agreed that I would be with him until he's discharged so I'm even spending the nights up there. If you need to reach me, text is best and I'll respond as quickly as possible," I tell her.

When she leaves, I jump in the car to drive back to Evergreen. I am still crying, and then I start shaking. I am having an involuntary flashback to the morning of November 2nd when Jim collapsed. I get flashes of moments: paramedics swarming around, frantic calls to get more help, the swirl of confusion and urgency, the dryness in my throat as I watched my husband slipping away...

I know that seeing his coat tossed aside is the trigger. I breathe and talk myself off the ledge again. *Be strong, Peg. You need to go back into the hospital ready to help Jim.* The 15-minute drive gives me time to cry all my tears out, get my head straight, and calm and center myself.

As soon as I enter Jim's room, though, I can tell by the looks going around from Carlos to Cookie to Jodie to Jim that something bad just happened.

"What is it?" I say, not wanting to go to worst-case scenarios, although I'm starting to.

I quickly learn that a respiratory therapist had come in while I was at home. Dr. Landover, the head of the Acute Rehab Unit, had previously told us she'd be coming. The respiratory therapist stops by to conduct an oxygen test in order to determine if a patient needs to be sent home with oxygen.

But apparently, all did not go well.

Jim says in his best angry whisper, "This idiot of a woman came in, said she was testing my oxygen levels, removed the oxygen out of my nose, and left the room. I just watched my oxygen levels dropping and started to panic. If she cared so much about me, why the hell didn't she stay in the room and watch my oxygen levels? This is unacceptable, and it makes no sense to even test me, as I'm days or even weeks from being discharged."

Jodie sighs. "Cookie and I weren't able to react fast enough to get the nurse," she says apologetically. "The respiratory therapist came in and didn't really explain much to us. She just told Jim we needed to do this test, took his oxygen out, and left the room. She said the test would run for 20 minutes, and then she would come back in and turn the oxygen back on. Cookie and I should have said something or reacted faster when his oxygen levels started to drop. I'm so, so sorry, Peg."

Cookie finishes the story: "We ran to get the nurse and got the oxygen back in his nose and his levels started to rise again, but it wasn't before he panicked and got all agitated."

I'm livid. I look around, suck in a breath, and practically yell, "EVERYBODY OUT!"

Nobody hesitates. They all file out. I shut the door behind them and go to Jim and hold his hand. "Honey, I'm sorry this happened. I just wish I was here with you."

Internally, I'm seething. I get one shower every few days, and every time I leave, it's a shit show. *For God's sake, why does everything have to be so difficult?* I wonder.

I can see that Jim is scared. I silently curse the therapist who came in. It seems that she didn't look at Jim's chart to understand what he'd been through, but had simply treated this as another procedural item to check off her to-do list. This is where some understanding of where a patient is at energetically and emotionally would improve our healthcare system immensely. If she had known he had three cardiac arrests and high anxiety about dying she might have taken more time and seen Jim as a human not just a test. I try to bring myself back to the present so I can help Jim do the same. I feel my anger subside as I focus on my husband.

Jim looks up at me. "The last thing that I remember before I died was losing air, and this test brought everything back, Peg," he sighs. "I got so stressed when I watched my oxygen level drop to 94, then 90, then 84 at the ten-minute mark. She said this would be going for 20 minutes."

I smile despite myself. "You're a numbers guy, so I bet in your head, you realized you were going to dip below 80 before you hit the 20-minute mark," I respond.

Jim has a monitor that clips onto his finger and reads his oxygen levels. Because he has an analytical brain, he watches these numbers like a hawk. This is what Bunnie had to report to him the second night in the hospital every time he coughed. With every breath, cough, or sneeze, Jim is worried his oxygen level is going to drop to 20 again, which is the number he was at the first day. To me, this is irrational thinking, as we have been told several times that when a patient's oxygen level dips below 80, there is an alarm that sounds at the nurse's station. After this incident, though, maybe Jim has a reason to be paranoid.

I leave my place beside Jim and move to his feet and just run pure white light into his system for about five minutes. To "run light" I imagine being bathed in white light and then transferring it to Jim through my hands. This high vibration, pure offering of healing is all I can muster in my frazzled state, but I know it will help calm everything down for Jim internally.

I kiss Jim's cheek and tell him, "I'm going to open the door and let your family back in, so let's move on from this incident. They are here because they love you, and I know they feel bad about how this all went down."

"Jim, I am so sorry," Jodie apologizes again when they all come back into the room.

Jim is calm again and says, "It's OK. I'm hungry, so let's eat and regroup."

I'm happy that Jim is gradually getting his appetite back and seems to have a new craving daily. His family is all about food and culture, and Cookie is more than happy to have a job that will help her son heal. I go to the small refrigerator on the eighth floor and find a Tupperware container of rice pudding. Cookie has several dishes that are family favorites, and her rice pudding is at the top of the list. She also recently made a chicken and rice soup that she brought up on her last trip to the hospital. I can feel the tense mood easing as all of us sit and eat together, occasionally breaking the silence with a joke or some minutiae from the day...anything that brings a feeling of normalcy to this disorienting time.

After all of us eat lunch together, a nurse asks Jim, "Would you like to try and shower today?"

"I guess," Jim whispers.

I'm a little confused about how this is going to work, given that Jim is still hooked up to machines. He has three separate IVs at this point, and the liquid bandage is still hanging onto his neck from his IVC filter procedure.

"This ought to be fun." I smile at Jim. He raises an eyebrow and nods.

A male nurse named Ayo shows up with a new hospital gown, a stack of towels, liquid soap that doubles as shampoo, and what looks like Saran Wrap sheets.

"This is going to take some doing," Ayo tells Jim as he begins to cover all of my husband's IVs with large, sticky, clear Saran Wrap adhesive bandages.

"Jim, hold still while I put this one on your neck." Ayo continues to work to get my husband covered up so he doesn't get anything wet that shouldn't be. Ayo then looks at me. "Peg, you and I are going to go into the bathroom with Jim, and since he's not strong enough yet to stand, he will shower sitting down on the stool I put in there. I have a walker he can push to help get him to the bathroom, and I will need your help guiding him and making sure he doesn't fall. You also need to make sure he doesn't get tangled in his oxygen tubing or IVs."

"Sounds daunting," I say under my breath, wondering how we are going to pull this off.

Ayo tells Jim, "Let's get you sitting up and on the edge of the bed."

Jim moves slowly and carefully. He's still weak, and I worry he might pass out. He swings his feet off the edge of the bed and winces as he moves. Ayo moves the oxygen machine and IVs into position so they are out of the way of the six feet of floor we have to traverse to get Jim into the shower. He steadies Jim and helps him stand, moving to the right side of the walker as I move to the left. I try not to laugh out loud thinking of how ridiculous this all is. I will never again take for granted my ability to stand while showering.

We make it to the bathroom and get Jim situated on the shower stool. "Here," Ayo says as he carefully helps Jim undress, then gives him the hand-held nozzle from the shower. "Let me get the water the right temperature for you."

Jim lets out a contented sigh as the first wave of warm water hits his body. He is struggling to wash his hair and not get water in the oxygen that is still in his nose.

"Can I help you?" I ask. Jim shakes his head no, his stubbornness surfacing again. Ayo is very kind and patient as Jim washes his arms and torso, then helps him stand so he can wash his legs. We find new bruises on Jim's back that make me cringe. I realize they match the raised pattern of our hallway rug that Jim was lying on as he received CPR. Jim's body isn't regulating very well, so he starts to shiver as soon as he's done and Ayo turns the water off.

"Let me help you," I insist. Jim lets me take over drying him off and getting his new gown on. He gets some more free waxing of his arm and neck hairs when we rip the plastic Saran Wrap bandages off his arms and neck. It looks like he managed to stay dry! Another victory!

"Jim, let's head for the chair because it's closer, and then they can change your bed and get you fresh linen," Ayo says.

We exit the bathroom and Jim makes it the few steps to the chair. Just like that day in the CCU when he got from the bed to the chair, it's like he has run a marathon.

Jim's oxygen level dips and his heart rate elevates with any type of exertion.

If there's one thing I like about the hospital, it's hot blankets on demand. The nurse grabs two for Jim to get him warmed back up, and puts all his tubes and IVs back in their proper place.

"I'm so tired," Jim yawns. I comb his hair so it doesn't dry funny, then open the door and let Jim's parents and Jodie back in the room.

"Quite an ordeal to shower someone all hooked up to machines, isn't it?" Jodie asks me.

"I'm glad we managed, but now Jim's exhausted," I reply.

All the same, I am excited about how far we have come in one day. I take photos of Jim with his mom and dad; despite his tiredness, he attempts a smile. I know he's glad that we're all here, and that it's helping him get through the scarier parts.

All the while, the bleeding is slowing down and his body is healing. Yesterday I felt so broken. It seemed like no matter what anyone did medically or energetically, I was going to lose my husband. Today, Jim is progressing on his healing path, and that's all that matters.

Stephani's husband, Erik, comes by to take Jim's parents and Jodie back to our house. Jodie and Bunnie are flying home tonight. Upon realizing that my night shift buddies are leaving, I feel my eyes well up with tears.

"I'll miss you terribly!" I say as I wrap my sister-in-law in a hug. "Thank you so much for coming and being here with us. I love you."

"I love you, too! Don't hesitate to reach out if you need anything," she says. "I'm just so glad we could be here for you...and I think he's going to make it." She gives me one more tight squeeze.

I pull up a folding chair next to Jim after Jodie and his parents leave and snuggle into his shoulder—gently, of course. Even though I'd prefer to be in a happier place with my husband—maybe in a vineyard in Napa kicking our feet up over a glass of wine—I am grateful for our moments of togetherness, which now seem so few and far between, given the number of people milling around at any given moment.

"I love you, and I'm glad you smell nice again," I jokingly say.

He laughs and closes his eyes to nap after what will probably go down as the most difficult shower he has ever taken.

I haven't had a chance to work on Jim since this morning, and do what I call a "check in." Once I've been working with a client for at least ten or more sessions I find I have a strong connection with their energy system. For me it's like looking in an energy field crystal ball. I connect, ask spirit to see their chakras and aura, make a few adjustments, then disconnect.

I run rose-colored light as I let Earth energy flow through me- pink light represents love and deep healing. Jim's energy field is wavering but feels the most solid I've felt it in six days. As hard as this has been for both of us, we are a team. I feel almost content as I let it sink in: Jim is going to live, and our family is going to remain intact.

I work for 15 minutes, and then go lie down on the bench to rest. As night fades to morning and all the days blur together, my exhaustion levels are reaching new highs. I have learned from experience how important self-care is, but in this situation, I will take what I can get. Catnaps are working for now.

Jim and I both wake up when another phlebotomist comes in to take more blood, and just as they finish, our friend and Wendy's husband, Myron, stops by. I glance at the clock and see it's 4 p.m.

"Wow, Jim, you've improved leaps and bounds in six days!" Myron says excitedly.

"Thanks for coming by; it means a lot to me," Jim whispers.

Wendy knows from one of my texts that the hospital is cold, so she bought three soft fleece jackets for me. Myron hands them to me, along with a hot chai tea latte.

"I need to get home for dinner and kids' activities, so I can't stay," Myron says apologetically. "I've talked to your boss, Jim, and he understands the situation. Peg, a woman named Fran is your contact to set up short-term disability for Jim and his leave from work."

Given the many pieces of information that are floating around in the air, I am so happy that there are other people holding and taking care of some of it. I'm certain I wouldn't have been able to do it on my own.

"OK, I'll get to that when I can. Thank you, and give Wendy a giant hug from me. We know that everyone is holding our family close, and we feel very loved."

A short time after Myron leaves, my sister, Sara, arrives with Thai food and a bag of goodies for me to eat. She was on vacation in Mexico when Jim collapsed, so this is the first time she's seen Jim. "I'm so glad you're still here with us," she says through her tears.

"Thank you for getting dinner for me. I'm so glad you're home from your trip. Did you have fun?"

"We did, although it was hard to be there, knowing that you needed me to be here with you," she admits.

Sara is one of the few people in my life who really gets me. Because she is six years younger, she was only 19 when Logan was born and spent 11 years with my children before she got married and had her own kids. She lives in Kirkland near Aunt Peggy. We have shared daily phone calls and support for each other in our journey as women and mothers for 20 years. We don't even call each other by name; we are both just "sister." The relationship is that primal.

"How are the kids doing? What do you need me to help with?" she asks, getting right to the point.

"Madison needs some attention. She's dropping assignments right and left, and broke up with her boyfriend! Oy! I believe I have the rest covered. I hired Blake to be our nanny in the afternoons and evenings until she gets a real job."

"What about your flight to California in a week? Should I cancel that for you?" Sara asks.

"Oh crap, I had forgotten about that!" Just ten days before Jim collapsed in our front hallway, my cousin Phil was diagnosed with a glioblastoma, or brain cancer. Life feels pretty cruel and jarring right now.

"Yes! Can you please cancel that and sync up with Madison? Those are the two most important things right now. The kids are arriving soon, so maybe talk to Madison when she gets here."

At that moment, our four kids come flying in the door. "Dad!" they scream, surrounding Jim in a flurry of hugs and conversation.

"These guys," I laughingly say to my sister, then go hug all of them.

I frown when I notice that Landon has a black eye. "What the heck happened?"

He shrugs it off. "It's not a big deal, Mom. I played with a friend of mine, and it happened, but I'm OK."

The other three look exhausted, but they assure me they're fine. I feel a pang of guilt over leaving them alone for so long, but I know they have plenty of support from the family and other people in our community. "You know what I just realized?" Sara says. "This is probably the first time you've all been together since November 2nd, so why don't I take a family photo of you guys?"

We all agree, and she snaps a photo of us on her iPhone. I feel joy flood through me as I glance at the photo. Jim looks battered but there is a light in his eyes again. I can see we are all tired from the stress, but I don't care— we are still a family. "Look at us! We've made it!"

My sister gives each of the kids a giant hug. "You guys have to promise to let me know if you need anything at all, especially you, Madison," she says before heading home to put her own kids to bed.

Jim and I take this opportunity to have a family meeting. As we gather around his bed, I do most of the talking, since Jim is still in whisper mode. I look at my kids, feeling so much love and gratitude for every single one of them, and simply for the fact that we all get to be here together. "Dad looks good, doesn't he?" They nod in agreement, and I continue, "I know it's been hard having both of us gone, but we need you to listen to Grandpa and Grandma, and do what they ask. I have Blake on board to be your afternoon nanny. Makenzie, that means she can help you get your driving time in for driver's ed, and take you and Landon to all your activities. I'm going to let you two talk with her and tell her what you need day to day. Obviously, I still need to be here with Dad."

"Blake?" Landon asks with an eager smile. "I *love* Blake!"

"That sounds great, Mom," Makenzie says. "I was wondering how I was going to get my driving time in. Are you sure I can drive with her, though?"

"She's over 21 years old, and given the circumstances, it's your only option," I say firmly. "Logan, I hope this will take some of the pressure off of driving your siblings around. You've been through a deep trauma and I want you to just work and sleep. Nothing more, nothing less."

"Thank God," Logan says with a frown. "I wasn't going to mention it, but I haven't been sleeping, and I've lost eight pounds in a week."

"Start eating Grandma's soup and I'll try and book you a therapy appointment as soon as I can," I tell him. I make a mental note to myself, not wanting to forget something this important in the midst of all that's happening.

I look at my older daughter, who isn't saying much. "Madison, you're quiet? Are you OK?" I ask.

"Yes, I'm just super tired," she responds. She is my most sensitive child, and although she doesn't voice her fears, I can tell by her recent dropping of assignments that she's starting to come undone. When she was little, I watched her closely when she started unraveling; it was way easier to deal with it if I addressed it quickly, rather than wait until she flipped what Jim and I called "the bozo bit." I sigh to myself. With my attention almost 100% on Jim and his condition, I don't have the time or energy to give to my daughter. I'm hoping that Sara will help with that.

Jim lets me know he has to go to the bathroom, since Logan brought him his favorite Vitaminwater Zero lemonade and he drank it all. I get my rubber gloves on and usher the kids out so he can pee in the bottle. In just a few minutes, I open the door to let them back in.

"Wow, Mom, you're like a nurse," Madison says, clearly impressed.

"Your dad needs an advocate, because things in the hospital can change hour to hour," I say, remembering the therapist debacle from earlier in the day. "Your dad and I agreed I would just come home to shower every couple days. We're hoping we're through the worst of it. This morning was a turning point, and now he just needs time to heal, because then they're going to move him to the Acute Rehab Unit once he's stable and the internal bleeding stops, before we bring him home. We don't know for sure when that will be."

"Mom, that's a long time in the hospital!" Landon exclaims, clearly distressed.

"I know, so I need all of you to be good to each other, and just remember why I'm here: to heal your dad. There are a lot of people all over the country praying for our family, and for your dad. So, I want you to ask any of our family, neighbors, or friends for help if you need it. We love all of you so much. I know none of this is easy. You guys are doing such a great job hanging in there."

I can tell that none of them had realized how bad it had gotten, since I had done my best to shield them from it. I can feel their mood turn somewhat somber, but I can also tell they've developed a newfound respect for their parents and the brave fight their father has been engaged in to live.

Jim whispers, "I love all of you. Probably time to head home since you have school tomorrow."

I soak up another round of hugs, and our kids leave. Without them around, silence quickly descends on us.

Jim yawns. "I feel pretty blessed, but I'm also exhausted. I think it's time to turn in."

I work with the nurse to get Jim settled in his bed and take up residence in the cursed chair next to him. This is my first night alone with Jim since he's been in the hospital. "This might just be our most romantic evening together yet," I tease. Jim nods off shortly after, and I take a moment to watch him breathe and check in on his field. Sometimes, when you work on someone and just start the energy moving in a healing direction, it's like a snowball rolling down a hill, picking up energy; the healing just continues rolling on its own. Instead of being scattered in pieces, Jim's field is the most whole and complete I have felt in six days. The layers of his field are starting to hold shape (they should mimic your physical body, with layer one being the closest to you) and some of his chakras are spinning. More energetic pieces of Jim are available for me to connect with, and I can feel him coming back to me. My mantra, "Love will get me through this if I surrender, allow, breathe," seems to be working.

I spend the next couple hours watching Jim breathe and doing reverse Reiki to combat the swelling and bruising all over his body. At 10:38 p.m. I text my brother Mike: "Jim's whole body shifts like an ocean wave when he breathes. Weird." The healer in me knows that this is his energy system and physical body trying to sync back up. It still feels like there is something I'm not quite seeing.

Think of nesting dolls when you think of layers of the field. Jim's nesting dolls still aren't coming together right.

I frown when I get Mike's response: "The struggle now is that the hospital has no idea what they are dealing with, Peg. Once you flatline a heart three times and the patient miraculously lives, there is not much known about patient physiology beyond what they know already."

I pause a moment to think about this. When are you clinically dead? At what point does your consciousness shut down? From what I've seen as a healer, and peoples' near death experiences I've read about, I believe you are in a suspended state for a short time after the heart flatlines. No matter what the doctors do or don't know, I have to stay true to myself as a healer.

My last thought before I fall asleep in my chair is one of gratitude. Jim and I have created a beautiful family, and there are many people who love us. There are folks praying for Jim across the country, many who don't even know him. I can't believe the striking difference between yesterday and today. Wendy's idea to put Jim's story on the Caring Bridge website has also helped generate energy that Jim has been using as fuel to heal, besides the work I've been doing. We always joke about my Aunt Patty having a direct line to Jesus, but after the turnaround this morning, maybe she really does.

I learned some valuable lessons this week about faith. You have to hold steadfast in your belief that something greater than yourself is in charge of the final outcome. Mike's text jarred me back to reality in that it showed me we still have a long way to go…and the journey has no roadmap. I have no idea what Jim's long-term outcome will be. I just need to keep doing what I'm doing, have faith and give the rest over to God.

Nine: Use the Force

At 3 a.m. I have an "aha" moment: *I need to ask other healers to work on Jim.*

I no longer have Jodie and Bunnie with me at night, which is hard, because I'd relied on their support, but it also frees me up to do more energy work. With other people in the room, I find it hard to focus, and if I can't drop in and find healer's aura, I won't be effective. Healer's aura is a space of grounded neutrality that readies me for healing someone without taking on their issues.

Last night, when I'd watched my husband's body heave like an ocean wave while he slept, I started to work to get his field back in balance. To be honest, I hadn't seen anything like it. I found it disconcerting to watch. At this stage in the game Jim's energy system is like a bowl on the pottery wheel, and with little nudges, guidance, and adjustments, I know I can mold it into the shape I want.

Right now, however, that is a long way off. I start small, charging Jim's feet and work on grounding him to the Earth through me. I believe that by holding the idea of a new thought as I'm healing someone, I'm inviting them to question their old belief systems and, therefore, shifting their energy flow and pattern. I think of it like I'm setting up a new energy path for my husband to become a part of, one where his body will reset and heal.

After I run some Earth energy and "invite" Jim's inner healer to embrace a new energy pattern, I check in on his right leg. Jim has been lying in bed, and all of a sudden, he lets out a scream. "Peg, my right leg feels like I'm being shocked with electricity, I have this intense pain zinging through it!"

Again, I hit new territory as a healer: What I'm seeing is a leg that looks like it has been fried, almost like he has suffered an electric shock. I heal the frayed edges but know it will be beneficial to have my healing school teacher, Alima, check in remotely and help me work on Jim's leg. I decide to text her when it's not three in the morning.

For most of the night that I am awake, I keep doing bits of energy work, as well as reverse Reiki on Jim's ribs, lungs, and all of his bruises. I leave the heart alone, though, as it feels like it just needs time and I don't want to interfere. Again, I am getting clear messages from the Divine on where to focus my attention and what would help Jim the most in the moment.

I can tell I am making progress, gently guiding and nudging Jim back into alignment. I can't do it for him, but I can work with the changing energy as he shifts. As happy as I am with his progress, it's becoming more and more evident that I need to get the word out to Alima and my healer friends about the specifics. But how? I immediately realize that Caring Bridge is the answer!

At 5 a.m., after Jim's first blood draw of the day, I post the following:

I almost peed my pants when Jim announced to the blood lady, "It's my birthday, I was born a week ago." Off a day but yes, he will now have two birthdays every year, 9/10 and 11/2. Your prayers, love, and intentions have carried Jim far. The dark and light duality in this journey are stunning. In total darkness one night, popping into the light the next. I would like to use Caring Bridge now as a place to give you specifics on what Jim needs for healing, for although I am captain of this crazy ship, I need a lot of crew.

For Jim:

1. He has been deeply traumatized and has a lot of fear, so please hold peace for his mind.

2. *His voice is gone, possibly from the vent or coughing. Pray that comes back. His whispering sexy voice is great but I like the old one better.*

3. *Massive bruising all over but especially his sternum and arms. Hold light.*

4. *His lungs are full of clots; imagine them loosening and clearing.*

5. *His left calf has a massive clot that we want to thin slowly over time.*

6. *They did intraosseous (jamming epinephrine into your bone marrow) on his right leg to start his heart so the wiring is all messed up, and he gets zinging pain. Pray that smooths out.*

7. *The internal bleeding has slowed but has not completely stopped, so pray that it does.*

8. *His system is still sorting out the blood thinner medication he will be on. Let it settle in today.*

9. *Jim doesn't trust yet that the IVC they put in him on Day 2 will hold the clots that may still break off from the calf clot. His testing/engineering brain finds flaws. Help him reach resolution.*

You can see the massive ocean we have to cross to get him back. If you don't like specifics, wrap him in love.

For Peg: I am a very weary captain, so just hold me up.

For our kids: Kindness, understanding, and love. At the moment, they have two parents engaged in quite a journey, and I am relying on the other people in their lives to be Mom and Dad.

For all our family members: Let them grieve and rail against this event that happened. And love them, a lot.

> *In much gratitude and love,*
>
> *Peg*

I know that by listing specifics, I will help the healers in my immediate circle to begin long-distance healing work on Jim. For everyone else, prayers or good intentions will help. I have faith that they are periodically checking Caring Bridge, since I have seen comments and prayers on the site throughout the week.

Around 7:30 a.m., Dr. Abernathy stops by early in her rounds. She has been checking Jim's progress daily and is delighted that he has not only survived, but is also recovering rapidly, given how severe his case is. As Jim talks to her, he gets one of those shooting pains down his right leg.

"Ah, oh my God!" Jim whisper-yells.

"What's going on?" Dr. Abernathy asks.

"I don't know what it is! I get this severe pain on the surface of my right shin. It's happening several times a day at random. It's like someone is rubbing steel wool on my right calf, shin, and foot. It lasts for only five seconds, but the pain is excruciating. What do you think is causing it?"

Soon, the grimace disappears off Jim's face and Dr. Abernathy rubs his leg and examines it.

"I don't see anything topical. I'm not sure where the pain is coming from," she says.

"This is the leg that they jammed the intraosseous (IO) into," I chime in. "Do you think it's from that?"

"Well, to be honest, most people who get the intraosseous aren't here to tell us about the experience. We don't have a lot of data collected about residual pain."

It takes me a moment before it clicks. The use of the IO is a desperate measure that they only use when they are out of all other options. Oh God. How on Earth is Jim *alive*?

"Well, I guess now you know there can be pain following the use of the IO," I tell her, not knowing what else to say.

"I think it will clear up within the week, but let me know if it doesn't. I need to continue my rounds. Dr. Young will be by later to discuss options for a long-term blood thinner. Good to see you, Jim," Dr. Abernathy says and quickly exits to attend to an entire hospital filled with patients.

I move to Jim's right leg and check in energetically to calm down the pain response. Jim leans his head back on the pillow and says, "I hope that this crazy pain goes away soon."

"I'm working on it, and I have been most of the night." I tell him. "I've sent the word out that I need more healers to work on you remotely. I think all of our efforts combined will help you heal."

I'm not sure yet if Jim has the same faith that I do that we can pull through this, but he nods. "I trust you, Peg. And I trust that we'll get the help we need."

Shortly after Dr. Abernathy leaves, I check my phone. I laugh when I see a text from Alima: "With your permission, I'm doing the things you requested."

I guess the universe started pinging her; without my even having to ask her directly, she had received my message from Caring Bridge that I needed help.

Alima had already put in her own personal growth work long before starting the healing school; she wasn't just asking us to do something without already blazing a trail for us to follow. She has become someone I trust implicitly, a mentor, and a valued friend.

The words "healing school" sound pretty innocuous in and of themselves, but Alima was, and is, fierce. When I was a student, she knew from her own experience what was needed to become a healer, and she was tough as nails. I really didn't think she liked me until after I was finished with the program and I continued to see her for personal healing work. Only then did she explain that when she pulled out what she called "the hammer" on me, it was just to challenge a belief system I held, and to accelerate my spiritual growth. In the moments I felt the hammer, I thought she must really hate me. All of this was worsened by the fact that she seemed to clearly have favorites, and I wasn't one of them. But my perspective changed when I was out of the school. From the other side, I could see that my idea about her having favorites was just my own insecurities seeping through—and her main objective was to push me to grow and heal my wounds.

I remember asking her, "Alima, why were you so hard on me in school?"

She just smiled and said matter-of-factly, "Because I saw that you had potential and were willing to do the work."

I raised an eyebrow. "But you were so nice to certain people in our class. I always thought you were playing favorites."

Alima laughed, a twinkle in her eye. "Oh goodness, no! The appearance of having favorites was because I gave up trying to get them to change. You, on the other hand? I knew you were making progress, even when it probably didn't feel like it." It was in that moment that my residual disdain and resentment towards her shifted to awe and gratitude.

Once I opened my practice and realized how well trained I am, I finally understood that all of Alima's "hammer" moments were part of the process of breaking down my ego so I could be a clear, neutral conduit of energy when doing healing work.

As my respect and admiration for Alima grew during my first year of practice, I asked her if she would spend one-on-one time with me, teaching me advanced healing techniques that we hadn't learned in class. This led me deeper into learning about things like bone bending (which allows you to get deep into the bones of your patients, energetically) and clearing out curses and entities (which sounds frightening but is truly about pulling out stuck energy, or literally "loving" it out of someone's system).

During my extra year of training with Alima, our relationship shifted to one of deep admiration for each other. Now, if there is anyone I want in my corner in a crisis, it's her.

I respond to her text: "Yes, calling all energy healers! Need lots of big kahunas like yourself for this one."

I want to give her specifics about the leg and what I'm seeing, so I text her the details: "The right leg that had the intraosseous, I see what looks like a copper wire scrubber for a leg. I've been slowly working the frayed bits down and trying to ground. I'm so tired—can you check in remotely? Permission granted."

The permission piece is an important part of energy healing, and one of the cardinal rules of being a healer is to always *ask* to work on someone. This allows you to go deep because the client is part of the decision, and just the "YES, I want to heal" is the first energy shift for them. They are the ones who get to decide that the energy pattern they are currently in is no longer working for them.

It is one thing to send out a blanket call for healers to help, but I know I need one or two specific healers to not only help Jim, but to be there for me after he has healed. Alima is obviously at the top of my list, but I have someone else I know will be perfect: Loretta Brown.

Julie, a friend who is also a client, had called earlier in the week asking if there was anything she could do for me. I text her back at 11:48 a.m. with my response: "OK, I've got one for you. Can you get Loretta on board? I'd like her to do 30-minute remote sessions once a week. Go to the CaringBridge.org page under Jim Rodrigues—the post today has my needs."

Loretta is a healer at Reiki Oasis, and someone I go to when I need healing. She has been in practice for years and is well respected in our field. Each healer has their own gifts, and Loretta is able to talk to spirit guides. She has helped me understand "why" some things happen, like in my session on November 1st, when I was trying to grapple with my cousin Phil's brain cancer diagnosis. Having loved ones get sick is one of the hardest things for me to grasp, because if the universe has a plan and everything is as it should be, then how do you explain a perfectly healthy 40-year-old man contracting brain cancer? I can only imagine her shock when she figures out that Jim collapsed the day after I saw her. I have a feeling she can guide Jim through his healing journey, and ultimately help me understand the "why" of November 2nd.

Julie responds a short while later: "Hi Peg. Of course. I have texted Loretta. The energy is in motion. I will let you know what she says. I am so sorry that all of this is happening. What a shock. My thoughts and prayers are with you and your family. Holding the light for you. Love, Julie."

An update comes minutes later from Julie: "Loretta has responded to my text. And she is happy to help you."

I sigh, relieved that I have two healers with more years of experience than I do working on Jim. I let out a little laugh, remembering that Jim affectionately refers to Alima as Yoda. He claims that she's straight out of *Star Wars* and that she is capable of crazy Jedi mind tricks. In this instance, he is correct. I can practically hear Obi wan Kenobi telling me, "Use the force, Peg." I have to remember my training, and who I am. My first response when Jim collapsed was shock and awe, but now I need to stand in my power and continue to use my abilities to bring him back...all the way back.

Jim's parents arrive at the hospital sometime in the late morning, all the days and hours are starting to blend together.

"How are you feeling today, son?" Carlos asks.

"Just exhausted but a little stronger. That shower yesterday felt pretty good. Exactly what the doctor ordered!" Jim tells his dad.

Although we've all been here with Jim the past week, these moments of truly recognizing how easily he could have slipped away creep up on us. And although having family around is helping to alleviate the stress, I still have to wonder how soon this entire ordeal will be over. How much more will Jim have to go through?

"Sorry, guys, but I have to go to the bathroom," Jim announces. Carlos and Cookie step out in the hall, and I go through our routine with the rubber gloves and pee bottle.

Only this time is different.

I let Carlos and Cookie back in, and with a beaming smile, I announce, "We have yellow urine!"

"Oh, thank God. This means the internal bleeding has stopped!" Cookie says excitedly.

It feels like Christmas in July. I am so happy I take a picture of the pee bottle sitting in the bathroom. Carlos and Cookie laugh at me, but they know what we have been through to get to this point.

This is a major milestone. Part of the exhaustion Jim is experiencing has to do with the fact that he has lost almost a third of his blood volume and has become anemic. His hematocrit hit 27 yesterday, the lowest it's been so far. In January, during his routine physical, Jim's hematocrit was at 40. He was due for a transfusion if he hit 22. After our amazing yellow urine moment, we all seem to be breathing easier. I send Jim's inner healer a quiet thank you.

I buzz the nurse and tell her excitedly when she comes in the room, "His urine is yellow!"

"Oh good," she says, "this means we can get him off the heparin drip and onto a blood thinner in pill form! I'll look into when we will be making that switch and let you know."

"Thank you so much," I say. "It'll be nice for him to be attached to one less machine!"

Jim's oxygen levels still go up and down, but now it's mostly related to exertion. He has started moving from the bed to chair regularly, and a physical therapist has come in a couple of times to see if Jim could use a walker. He can make it a few steps, but that's about all he can manage for the time being.

When he rests, he takes the oxygen off for small increments of time. It's like weaning a two-year-old off a bottle. The spirometer has helped his lungs start to recover, and his oxygen levels are starting to stay above 90. The doctors want to see a consistent 92 in order to fully take Jim off the oxygen. They can control the amount of flow of oxygen, so they have lowered his setting to a 1, which is the lowest.

Jim's yellow urine signifies that his kidneys are functioning, which tells me that his internal organs are beginning to heal. We're finally trending in the right direction!

I get a text from Alima: "I've been focused on you and your requests. Lots of bubbles for you…use them."

Ah yes, bubbles!

This is something we learned in the healing school: When someone is struggling or needs extra care, you can float them bubbles of energy to use as needed. I love that she is sending bubbles of energy to me now, and just knowing this makes me more secure. I can feel those bubbles coming in, and I'm grateful. I need them, especially since exhaustion is starting to seep into my bones.

I look down at my phone and see I have another text, this time from Kelly. "How can I help?"

I text her back: "I need adrenal support. Would your naturopath see me here?"

I know that Kelly's naturopath will make house calls. I can feel how taxed my system is, and six nights of very little sleep and standing on the hospital floor all day have taken a serious toll on my body. Energetically, I am in tune and my entire being is focused on healing Jim, but the human part of me feels like shit. As a healer, I'm powerful beyond measure, but I know that will only get me so far. I also have to take care of my human needs, and this week, that's an area where I've been failing.

Dr. Young stops by in the early afternoon. "Wow, Jim, you look great," he remarks. "In my entire career, I have never seen anyone recover as quickly as you have."

I silently wonder if all the energy work I've been doing behind the scenes has contributed to that.

"Well that's good news!" Jim smiles.

"Jim, you've got a few options for a blood thinner. The name is deceiving. They don't actually thin the blood, but rather, suppress the body's clotting ability. Because you had a DVT develop from knee surgery, you are now considered high risk for clots. We want to prescribe a blood thinner to reduce the risk of more clots forming," Dr. Young explains.

Jim nods. "OK, let's do it, then!"

"You have a few choices for medications. The most common is Coumadin, but the problem there is that you have to continually monitor yourself as you adjust to the medicine, which would mean more blood draws in a lab." Jim wrinkles his nose at that news. I frown, too; his arms look like pincushions from the continuous blood draws.

"I can see by your reaction that Coumadin isn't your first choice," Dr. Young says. "There are many new drugs that have no dietary restrictions and don't require the blood draws, as they automatically regulate how much clotting they reduce. The one I'm thinking would be best for you is Xarelto."

"That sounds like a good option...right?" Jim asks.

"It is, although be forewarned that Xarelto doesn't reverse as quickly as Coumadin."

Jim and I take a few minutes to deliberate. If Jim were to need emergency surgery, he could bleed to death before they could reverse the effects of the Xarelto...but we decide we'll have to take the risk. We both trust what Dr.

Young is saying. "The Xarelto seems like the best option for now," I tell him. "Jim is wondering if he will be on it for the rest of his life?"

"Once the DVT in your calf thins out and goes away, we can get you off the Xarelto," Dr. Young assures my husband. "We would probably schedule an ultrasound on your left calf about three months from now to check the progress."

"Do I have to wean myself off Xarelto slowly, or is it automatic?" Jim asks.

"It's immediate—you would just quit taking your medication. Let's plan to get you off the heparin drip this evening and switch to the Xarelto pill." When Dr. Young leaves, Carlos and Cookie ready themselves to take off and have dinner with the kids at home.

Jim has some of his mom's homemade chicken and rice soup for dinner, topped off with rice pudding, and settles into bed for the night. Just by looking at him, I can tell he's coming back into his body after being gone for so long. His eyes look brighter and the ocean wave breathing pattern has shifted and normalized. My husband is *here* with me.

I text Alima an update at 5:40 p.m.: "Well, your efforts worked, everything turned today. Love you, big kahuna energy healer."

I think back to the events of the day and smile at my recollection of seeing the yellow urine. I feel like Rocky Balboa reaching the top of the steps. Victory!

At 9 p.m. the night nurse comes in with Jim's pain meds and the Xarelto in pill form. I take a picture of the heparin machine—or as I call it, the "heparin bitch"—to give it a proper goodbye. I text my brother the photo and an update: "Just said goodbye to this evil machine."

If I was exhausted a few hours ago, I am *really* tired now. I have the strength to do a short healing on Jim before getting a little sleep. I always start at his feet to ground him since this is what we learned in school. You have to establish an earth energy connection to layers one through three, before you can make changes above in layers four through seven. Once I get hands on, I can see that Jim's right leg has greatly improved.

Thank you, Alima, I say silently to myself.

All the copper wires are tucked back in and I can sense smaller zings and zaps as Jim's right leg regains energy through his foot chakra. The flow through his whole system is smoother. I gently run healing light into his kidneys and liver, and I offer a silent thank you to his body for working so hard this past week. I can tell every organ in his body is shocking. I think back to when this all began; every time Jim coded, his organs shut down and restarted. It's almost like they are confused now...are the lights on or off?

You can sew or repair the layers of the field, and by doing so, create a template so the organs know their place. I do this for Jim now to calm his internal organs down and guide them back to their normal flow and rhythms.

During a healing, you have to take direction from a client's inner healer. I can tell that Jim's is telling me, "I NEED TIME."

I can also sense Jim's system has had enough, so I quickly finish work and tell my husband, "I need to get a little sleep. This has been a good day, all things considered."

"A *very* good day," Jim says. He looks at me, cocking his head a little bit. "I can tell how tired you are, honey. Are you OK?" Now that Jim has stopped peeing blood, his anxiety has gone down and he can focus on other things. I smile at his concern. Here he is just six days out from three cardiac arrests, and he's asking me if *I'm* OK?

"I'm hitting the wall, but I definitely feel better that I have a support team working on you, and I'm going to see if the naturopath can give me a B12 shot when I see her." I laugh. "You know me. I always take care of everyone else first, and then wonder why I get sick. I'm hoping to prevent that because you need me here."

"Whatever you need to do, honey," he says lovingly. "You've been a superhero. I can see how tired you are." He sighs. "I know this whole experience has been pretty intense, and I just want it to be over for all of us."

The night nurse comes in for one last check on Jim's vitals. Suddenly, another nurse pops her head in and asks Jim: "Bobby, are you allergic to anything other than Brazil nuts?"

Jim and I look at each other, stunned. Who the hell is Bobby? Jim just smiles politely and replies, "Nope."

Luckily, our night nurse goes after her to inform her that Jim isn't Bobby. (God forbid the real Bobby is actually allergic!) Jim and I bust a gut. It's a simple moment, but we both need a little comic relief.

We fall asleep holding hands. "Good night, Peg, I love you," Jim says.

"I love you too, Bobby," I reply, smiling.

Ten: The Crash

I fall asleep joking about Brazil nuts but abruptly wake up to what sounds like Jim choking on one.

Oh, for crying out loud!

I sigh and turn over on the recliner. I don't like being this impatient with my hospitalized husband. I know it's not his fault...but I am *so* sick of the incessant coughing, beeps, and antiseptic hospital atmosphere that I feel myself slowly sinking into a dark place. I'm a fish out of water here. I have always been a positive, glass-half-full person, so this is new territory I'm entering. I feel like I am on a battlefield and don't know what enemy is lurking in the shadows. I am irritable and moody—a state of mind I don't generally experience. I know I have PTSD after what happened to Jim, but what I'm currently experiencing feels far more sinister. I need help, and fast.

It's 2:28 a.m. in the wee hours of November 9th, seven days since Jim's collapse, and the beginning of my crash. The proverbial straw that broke the camel's back. The downward spiral I'd been keeping at bay now seems to be surging up toward me. I had held myself together, held myself together, held myself together...until I no longer could...

I sit there in the darkness, my brain feels listless and muddled, and my energy is beginning to fracture. I know I need help.

My brother is more intuitive than he realizes, and it's like he can sense I'm starting to crack. He texts me all night—offering encouraging words, a photo of a virtual hug, funny jokes. Even though my mental state is in question, I can at least feel how much my brother loves me.

At 2:36 a.m. I text Mike about the minutiae of the day: "When we switched off the heparin to Xarelto, his urine went back to Kool-aid. They said it can happen: three pees, the color is the same."

Is this what my life has come to—texting my brother about my husband's urine?

His response does little to reassure me: "Jim's physiology is in uncharted territory—you need to recognize that he was dead three times. The trauma involved with bringing him back to life is nearly unprecedented. I am certain it has happened before but it is a very unique scenario. Transferring off one medicine to another impacts Jim's organs, particularly his kidneys. Additionally, every reaction is unknown right now. The best thing to do is wait and pray, Peg. I know you don't want to hear that, but I expect Jim's caregivers at the hospital truly are monitoring and hoping all things stabilize over time."

I am totally awake now. I know he is right...and I also know that much of the East and West Coast is praying for Jim. I have my tribe of lightworkers involved and have listed specifics for what I need. I believe that with clear intentions, love, and prayers, anything is possible. And we have already experienced one miracle: Jim is alive. Still, how much more can I handle? After the high I felt seeing yellow urine and then having it switch back to Kool-aid again, I can feel my faith being sorely tested...and I am tired, bone-weary exhausted. Even though we had a great day, I know Jim still has a long road ahead to achieve a full recovery. And that, just maybe, I am no longer in any condition to help.

Again, I remind myself to surrender to the moment. I recite my mantra in my head a few times: *"Love will get me through this if I surrender, allow, breathe."* It does little to reassure me.

I sit up in the recliner and breathe deeply. I chide myself: *Come on, Peg, your mantra is working, and you can do anything. Look at how fast Jim is healing!*

Nope—still not working.

In energy healing, there is something I call the "magic line." Energy has an unseen power; anything above the magic line is positive energy; anything below, negative. The problem is, when you sink below the line, it's like you get stuck in a tornado of "bad" energy and it's hard to pull yourself out on your own. Once you can pop yourself above the line, you are in a love updraft and life floats along pretty nicely, at least for a while. Then a major life event occurs, and you dip below the line again.

I am sinking. I know I have fallen below the line. There is no one to help me in the middle of the night—no one, that is, but my brother. I realize that because my brother is an EMT, he can answer questions about some of the medical speak I have heard and not understood so far. I text him: "Dr. Abernathy said they don't have a lot of patients alive to talk to after an IO."

He gives me more information about the IO and the internal bleeding: "Know when the paramedics go IO, that shit just got real. Hypo = low. Hyper = high. In all things medical, it pays to learn Latin. So, when you bleed internally, your volume of blood drops. If it drops too low (hypo), the body begins shutting down—right now my guess is the docs are carefully trying to stabilize Jim's volume of bleeding to keep his system from shutting down.

His kidneys are taking the brunt of that stabilization along with his liver."

Me: "They did an ultrasound of kidneys and bladder. They look great, heart looks great. Clots bullshit."

Mike: "Right now it sounds like his lungs are in jeopardy with the clots. The heart is bruised and has an umbrella. Now it is up to his liver and kidneys to shoulder the load, thus the blood in his urine."

Me: "I'll do energy work on his liver. I just have to think…if he made it this far—totally fucked up if we lose him now."

My despair shifts quickly when the nurse comes into the room and interrupts my crash course on medical terms from my brother.

She announces, "My name is Wei."

Jim's quick response is, "Where's Will?

I laugh out loud. *Where there's a will, there's a way.* His impish humor is what rallies both of us in dark times, and since we can laugh our way through it, deepens our love for one another. Jim smiles, settles back into his pillow, and nods back to sleep.

Mike sends more words of reassurance: "Keep everything positive and take it one step at a time. Things will go well, then back to shitty—the ride is underway.

Hell, he is already a medical miracle—if he survived all that trauma, this current challenge is a walk in the proverbial park! All my EMS [Emergency Management Services, which include police, fire, and medical personnel] friends are floored he survived three codes—not one of them has ever had a survivor after three."

I realize I still don't know the exact details of what it took for the paramedics to get Jim back.

I know I can continue to ask all these stupid questions of my brother without shame, so I write: "The heparin and Xarelto break up the clots, but then where do all the broken-up clot pieces go?"

Mike clarifies: "Absorbed back into his system—that actually may be the reason his urine turned to Merlot again. I suggest asking the doc today if the reason his urine changes colors is due to his kidneys processing the clots."

Somehow this thought reassures me, especially since it's a possibility that the doctors hadn't even informed me about. I marvel at Mike's knowledge and realize there's a lot that I don't know. Maybe Jim isn't internally bleeding, but just processing the clots out of his system. The night nurse mentioned that when you introduce a new anticoagulant, some new bleeding can happen.

I explain to Mike why I'm still awake at 3:20 a.m. "He's coughing up his guts tonight. No sleep for sister. I'm texting you and monitoring him."

I am starting to nod off sitting up but am learning the art of sleeping in snatches. "Going to sleep for five. Love you, brother."

Mike responds: "Take care of yourself—caregivers need as much love and support as the patient! LOVE YOU!"

The night is a dark, lonely abyss that Jim fights against as soon as the light of day fades. I have felt myself slipping into that abyss all night and know I need help. After my text conversation with Mike, I am fully aware that I am not OK. I know my job in this moment is to heal my husband, but I can't do that on empty.

I move to the bench and fall asleep so hard that when the nurse wakes me up at 6 a.m., I'm talking in garbled speech. Now I am highly concerned about myself, and I can tell that the nurse is, too. I feel like I am having a stroke. I intuitively know it's just my system finally letting down after a week of deep trauma and fighting for my husband's life.

Yes, that's all.

I rouse myself and stretch, and then, knowing I need my relief crew to show up, text Cookie at 6:07 a.m. "We got off heparin around 9 p.m. and took Xarelto pill at the same time, which will be once a day. Since then, the urine is back to red. Jim is coughing, agitated, and anxious. He had 2 Oxycodone at 6 a.m. What time are you coming? I need my dad to drive me home. Crashed hard last night. No strength in me today. I might need 4–5 hours of sleep."

Cookie calls me back around 8 a.m. "We will be up around 9 to 9:30 a.m," she tells me. "Your dad took Landon to school, and then is coming back to bring us up to the hospital. I think it's a good idea that you go home and rest."

"Mmmhmmm," is all I can mumble, "see you soon." And I hang up.

I see a text from my brother: "How is Jim doing now?"

My response shows how much I need a break "He's crabby and I'm tired and feel like telling him to fuck off." It's true, and I don't even feel guilty saying it.

Mike: "Best go to a spa and decompress, sister."

Me: "I am going home to sleep. Hit the wall last night."

Mike's humor cracks me up: "Hit the fucking wall already, the brake is on and the tires are on fire."

That isn't what I had been thinking about my state of being, but now that he mentions it, I can see that it's pretty darn accurate. This part of healing has always been the hardest for me: self-care.

My parents show up with Jim's parents, and I can tell they know I'm crashing. My dad once came to my rescue in college when I was horribly sick with bronchitis. I'm reminded of that feeling now, when you are so out of it that you can't even lift your head to say, "I need help." You just need someone to intuit it, then come in and carry you out.

I go to say goodbye to Jim. "I love you, honey, but I need rest and am not sure when I'm coming back up. Your parents will stay with you all day."

"Go! I can tell you need it," Jim responds.

My dad helps me pack my bag, and just like when I was 19 years old, leads me out to the car with his eyes full of concern. My mom is quiet and gently pats my arm.

I unleash a torrent of tears as soon as the car door slams shut. "I can't do this anymore! I can't. I want out. I want to quit."

My sister has a spidey sense that allows her to always pick up on when I'm in trouble. Unsurprisingly, she calls on my way home from the hospital. Just hearing her voice, I snap and let out a wail like a wounded animal: "I'm so tired. I don't know if I have anything left to give!"

She quickly assures me, "Don't worry, Sister, I'll take care of everything."

My parents are tearing up in the front seat as they listen to me speaking with Sara. I know that as hard as this is for me, their hearts are breaking at the sight of their daughter. All they can do is let me cry. When we pull up to my house, they guide me upstairs and into my bed. I literally start to convulse and shake, again feeling like I am having a stroke. I feel my mother kiss me on the forehead, and at some point, I fall into a restless sleep.

I wake up to find Madison lying next to me, her head close to mine, her eyes big. "Are you OK, Mom?"

At first, I am confused about where I am and have to sift through my brain to reorient myself. I sigh and allow myself to cuddle up against my daughter. I feel like her child, small and worn out.

"Mom, are you OK?" she asks again.

I reach out to stroke her hair out of her eyes. "No, but I will be. My system is taxed, and at some point, your physical body has to shut down when it's gone through a lot. Mine shut down today."

"What happens now?" she asks in a sweet but slightly scared voice.

"I got some sleep and need to eat something nutritious to get my body working again. Can you go ask Grandma what's been delivered?"

She heads downstairs to ask my mom what our friends and neighbors have brought to the house.

"How about a warm lentil cassoulet?" she yells from downstairs.

"Yes, please! Can you ask Grandma to warm it and bring it up to me?" I call out.

"Grandma's on it," she tells me as she comes back into the room.

I look at my normally reticent daughter and wonder what's been going on while I've been gone. "Are *you* OK, Madison? I know it's been a long week."

She plops down on the bed. "Yeah, I guess so...I got a speeding ticket last week the day after Dad collapsed. I guess I was distracted and not paying attention," she says apologetically, searching my eyes for a reaction.

I'm too worn out to get mad. I smile at her reassuringly, realizing that this is probably the reason she was so quiet when she came to visit Jim and me in the hospital recently. "That's fine—we'll try and get it reduced in court."

My mom shows up with the cassoulet, and she and Madison both sit on the bed as I eat. I swear, it's the best meal I've had in my life. I can feel the warmth of the food fill my physical body and my soul.

I finish eating and tell my mom, "Thank you. I think I have enough strength to try and shower now."

I reassure Madison, who still looks concerned. "I'm going to be all right, honey. I hope I didn't scare you. This has been really tough on me, and on all of us. Thank you for helping around the house and staying on your normal schedule. More than anything, I think maintaining our routines is going to help us get through this."

Madison smiles. "You bet, Mom. I'm going downstairs to have Grandpa help me with my chemistry homework."

I crawl out of bed and into the bathroom, peel off the clothes that have been stuck to my skin for a couple days, and start the water. These occasional hot showers are the best. Aside from the lentil cassoulet that is still warming my belly, that is. I dry my hair and pause a moment to recite my mantra: "Love will get me through this if I surrender, allow, breathe." I hear a quiet "Amen" from deep within me.

My inner resolve and will are back. Sleep and food are magic.

Once I get new clothes on, I'm a brand-new woman. I head downstairs and realize my new console and bench have arrived—probably when I was in the hospital. I see my lamps on the floor and take a moment to unwrap them and plug them in. My dad joins me. "Is there anything I can do?" he asks.

"I just want to take a moment to reacquaint myself with my house. Can you help me get light bulbs in these lamps? They're in the laundry room cabinet."

My dad and I work together to get the lamps plugged in and a couple pictures hung on the wall. We work together quietly and efficiently. He knows this is important in some way, so he doesn't question me. I need to feel normal. Just a normal housewife, doing normal things...that's me. I feel a laugh burble up from deep within as I contemplate the weirdness of that word, *normal*. What does it even mean anymore?

"Are you feeling better?" my dad asks. "It's nice to hear you laugh again."

I think of how grateful I am for my parents. "Thank you for saving me, Dad," I say quietly. "Do you remember when you drove five hours to Washington State University after you'd worked a full day at school, loaded me in the car, and drove another five hours to get me home? That meant the world to me. Kind of felt like that again today."

His eyes tear up a little and he folds me in a big dad hug. I breathe him in, allowing myself to just be held. To not have to keep the weight of the world on my shoulders, but to share it with someone else. "I love you, Peg," he says, his voice heartfelt. "You are a strong, amazing woman."

I glance at the clock and realize it's almost 2 p.m. "I need to get back up to Jim," I say to my dad. When I notice the look of consternation on his face, I hold up my hand and say, "It's really OK. I feel ready now."

I text Cookie so she doesn't worry: "Jim want anything? Heading back up."

"They are moving him to rehab today" is her response.

"Good, I'm on my way," I reply.

I head upstairs to pack fresh clothes, some warm socks, face wipes, and hair ties. As my parents take me back to the hospital, I send two texts. One is to my girlfriend Maureen, who is still on a search for a therapist for Logan and me. "Really need that therapist. I am shocking bad and starting to act like I am having a stroke." The second is to Alima: "Moving Jim to rehab today. Would you be able to come up and settle my system down tomorrow?"

I arrive back at the hospital to find Carlos and Cookie packing up the room to move him to the Acute Rehab Unit (ARU).

Jim immediately looks at me. "Thank goodness, Peg. I was worried about you. Are you feeling better?"

I look at my husband. All traces of my previous irritation from the morning are gone. All I see is someone I love who needs me. "I am now. I just needed some sleep and a good hot meal."

"I'm glad," he says excitedly. "I got off oxygen today. They were watching my levels carefully, and I never dipped below 92. The spirometer seems to be doing its job to heal my lungs. I can take deeper and deeper breaths."

"I am so happy you had a good day and weaned yourself off the oxygen! This is another milestone reached, and one step closer to going home." An aide comes with a wheelchair and helps transfer Jim from the bed. Jim still isn't strong enough to walk on his own, but I hope the physical therapy at the ARU will take care of that. The aide wraps him in a warm blanket and leads the procession out of our eighth-floor penthouse. After meandering through the hallways and taking a short elevator ride, we arrive at the ARU.

If his old room is a penthouse, his new room in the ARU is a broom closet. It's tiny, cramped, and has a bathroom that Jim will have to share with his neighbor. I gaze up at the fluorescent lights and frown. I can see that we have been completely spoiled on the eighth floor. The one advantage down here is a big kitchen and common room where our family can hang out. When we all go into his new room, Jim, Carlos, Cookie, and I are packed in like sardines.

I text Logan to come by and bring Carlos and Cookie home now, and then ask if he can come back later with his brother and sisters. After Jim's parents leave, I look around. Jim and I still haven't seen a nurse or been told what's in store for him now. "Maybe they don't know we're here?" I ask Jim. "Should I go find someone?"

He shakes his head. "No. I'm sure they must have a lot going on, so let's just relax. They'll get here." I nod. Given that we are no longer in an emergency state where Jim's future is completely dependent on doctors taking action in the moment, I can appreciate my husband's more relaxed demeanor.

A short while later, a physical therapist shows up with an orchid and poster from Jim's work. He shakes my hand and says, "Welcome to the ARU! My name is Chuck. I'm one of the therapists here. We have patients moving in and out right now, so I'm sure the nurse assigned to you will be in shortly."

I settle in and check my phone. I see a text from my sister, Sara: "How's the rest of the day? Sending love."

I smile, glad my sister is back in town for our daily check-ins. "You caught me at my wall. Or what Mike called my implosion."

I groan to myself when I notice that right next to Jim's bed is a giant recliner chair. I don't think the hospital ever intended for family members to sleep in that chair for a night, let alone a week. I get everything put away, and a nurse finally shows up.

"Hello Jim, welcome to the ARU," she says enthusiastically. "It's probably a little smaller than your last room, and that's because we don't want you in it. Our plan is to get you up and walking tomorrow. We are going to push you hard to get you home. Every day you are here, you will meet with three therapists: physical, occupational, and speech. You have a white board, just like you did on the eighth floor, but notice on the top right-hand corner we list your therapy appointments for the day. We still list your medications on the bottom right." Turning to me after her spiel, she asks, "Are you his wife?"

"Yes, I am. My name is Peg," I introduce myself.

"Nice to meet you, Peg. Tomorrow, the physical therapist will clear you to walk Jim around the unit, but for now, hit the call button if he needs to get up to use the bathroom."

"No more pee bottle?" I joke. "That sounds great!"

Jim interjects, "I just got off oxygen today but am a little nervous to go all night without it. Is it possible to have the tube hooked up and I can just put it into my nose if my levels start to dip?"

"No problem at all. Let me go get the tubing."

The nurse leaves, and Jim smiles at me. "I feel pretty good. Should we have the kids come up with Logan for a quick hello?"

I text Logan that now would be a good time to come up with all his siblings to see their dad. The nurse returns with the tubing and helps Jim to the bathroom and then back into the chair. He wants to sit up and look as normal as possible. (There's that funny word again...I think we need a new one.)

All four kids come bursting through the door at 8 p.m.

"Hey, Dad!" they exclaim in unison.

Landon is happy to see Jim and says appreciatively, "Dad, you look more like yourself now! There aren't all these tubes and wires coming out of your mouth, nose, and arms."

Jim laughs. "I'll take that as a good thing," he says. "I have to do some therapy, but I hope to be home within the week!"

"Oh, good!" Landon exclaims, throwing his arms gently around his dad. "I've missed you so much!"

The kids talk to their dad for a bit about the minutiae of their own lives. Jim is a protective father and asks Madison somewhat jokingly, "So I heard you have a new boyfriend?"

Madison is a little embarrassed. "Yes, but don't worry, Dad—he's a nice guy!"

Jim's response is the same as when he asked about the last three boyfriends—a knowing "Mmmhmmm." Madison is a beautiful girl, and there has been no shortage of boyfriends. Luckily, they don't seem to last too long.

Logan and Makenzie chime in. "Don't worry, Dad!! We follow her on Instagram, so we'll let you know how things are going."

We all laugh together a bit more before I take the kids by twos and walk them into the common area of the ARU. The main purpose of the ARU is so victims of strokes, or anyone who is disabled, can rehabilitate fully by learning how to cook, eat, and navigate around furniture. They even have a room that is a real bedroom so that patients can learn how to get in and out of bed on their own. Although Jim isn't a stroke patient, he's going to need a lot of help to get back to his pre–November 2nd state. At this point, I'm not even questioning whether that's fully possible or not. I'm just feeling grateful that the last few days have resulted in so many dramatic shifts.

The kids are glad to see their dad, but given the tiny quarters, they're quick to take off. The night nurse comes back to check on Jim and give him his night meds. Jim's coughing still hasn't improved, so we increase the dose on the cough syrup. At this point, he is still trying to clear his lungs, so they want him to cough as much as possible during the day, but at night he needs rest to heal his body.

The nurse puts an oxygen monitor on Jim's finger so we can read the levels in case he dips below 90 and we need to put some oxygen in his nose. It also has an alarm that will sound if Jim falls asleep and his oxygen drops to 80. Because the ARU is so small, the nurse's station is directly across the hall.

"Peg, can we keep the door open just a little bit?" Jim asks me. This is also what he requested on the eighth floor, just so he didn't feel claustrophobic. I know he's in a better place, but his anxiety hasn't been quelled completely yet. I am grateful for a small curtain we have as a buffer. The room is so small and stuffy that we set up a fan to circulate air.

I get Jim settled in his bed and then make a nest in my new chair with as many pillows and blankets as I can. I feel like a dog spinning into circles before flopping down to sleep.

I think we are asleep for 30 minutes before the alarm on his oxygen monitor goes off, jarring both of us out of a deep slumber. "What the hell?" I say. The nurse comes running in, only to discover that Jim had rolled over and pulled the monitor off his finger.

I breathe a sigh of relief. Thank goodness.

We get a new monitor on, tape it down, then start to drift off again. I have my recovery plan in place. Maureen had texted me earlier in the day that she would find a therapist by Friday—and Alima has an appointment at Evergreen tomorrow, so she agreed to come by and see me.

I know it's time to allow everyone's prayers for Jim to carry me, as well. I haven't even had the strength to run energy on Jim this afternoon, and at this point, I believe I need more help than him.

I look up at the ceiling and think to myself, *When am I going to learn to take care of yourself first before you reduce yourself to nothing by giving all of you away?* I am still working on balance obviously, but I did go home and do some self-care.

Eleven: Tethered

I toss and turn and wake occasionally to Jim's coughing, but still manage to get the best night's sleep in the hospital I've had thus far.

I turn my attention to Jim as I hear him stirring. He slowly wakes up, rubbing his eyes before giving me a strange look. "Peg, in the middle of the night, you looked at me and said, 'If you don't stop coughing, I am going to let you code again.'"

"What?!! I did not!" I exclaim, mortified.

"You so did, but don't worry—it's pretty darn funny." I can't help laughing with Jim. Considering I hit rock bottom yesterday, I actually feel like there's nowhere to go but up.

Jim has three therapy appointments set up today: physical therapy at 10 a.m., occupational therapy at 1 p.m., and speech therapy at 2 p.m. We have been warned by nurses and doctors that the Acute Rehab Unit will push Jim hard. He is apprehensive about what his body can do, and I in turn am nervous for him. I know he must be tested to evaluate what effect the cardiac arrests and subsequent CPRs had on his body, but I'm worried about what they might find. What if there is some brain delay? I know my proud, stubborn husband will NOT be good with that.

The nurse comes in and asks, "Do you want some breakfast today?"

"I'll try some scrambled eggs," Jim says. I raise an eyebrow; there's a first time for everything. Jim has been eating bananas or tangerines for breakfast daily, so I'm glad he's adding protein. He's going to need his energy, given all these therapy appointments.

The nurse looks at Jim like she's readying him for some difficult information. "Today is going to be hard, and you will feel pushed to your limit, but I want you to hang in there, Jim," she says. "Take your time and do the best you can with the therapists. The whole point of the Acute Rehab Unit is to get you home, and we're going to do our best to help move you along and out of here as fast as we can."

Jim responds enthusiastically. "After the last few days, you're not going to hear me complaining! Besides, I think I did OK without oxygen last night, so that's an encouraging sign." he says.

My understanding of healing, both physically and energetically, is that it's a catch-22. You typically heal faster if you get moving and can clear out toxins, but you also don't want to push too hard, otherwise it sets you back in your healing. I'm not sure that I'm quite as enthusiastic as Jim right now; I'm concerned that all he's managed physically for the past eight days is a little bit of walking and not much else. And while he just weaned himself off oxygen yesterday, which tells me his lungs are stronger, how strong are we talking? Are the therapists going to push him too hard? I hold my breath and hope for the best.

Carlos, Cookie, and I have talked about their involvement now that Jim has moved to a smaller room in the ARU, and we agreed that I will continue to spend nights with him. Because I am getting more sleep, I informed them that I'm strong enough to handle the days, too. If they decide to visit and be with Jim during therapy, then that will be when I go home to shower.

At 10 a.m., a therapist arrives. She has a bright smile and carries herself in a confident, trustworthy way. I immediately relax, as my intuition tells me we are in capable, competent hands.

"Hi Jim, my name is Kim, and I'm one of the physical therapists here. There are three basic rules in the ARU. No falling, no falling, and no throwing balls through the walls."

Jim and I both laugh. "Do patients regularly throw balls through the wall?" I ask.

"Well, it's happened before, but honestly, the biggest concern is the falling," she reiterates. "To enforce the no-falling rule, Jim has to wear a gait belt around his waist whenever he's walking anywhere on our floor." She looks directly at him and says, "You are never, I repeat, *never*, to walk unassisted."

Kim shows us what looks like a large karate belt and then shows me how to buckle it around Jim's waist so it's nice and secure. "Now that you know how to put it on, I'll add you to the list of people cleared to walk Jim," Kim tells me.

"That sounds funny," I quip. "I get to walk my husband." I imagine myself pulling him down the hospital hallway like a pet on a leash, and I can't help but snicker.

"The next thing I'm going to get you is a wheelchair." Kim leaves and comes back with one. "You are allowed to take Jim around the hospital grounds, but we do *not* want him to get up and out of his chair."

"OK, that sounds great," I assure her. It's only been a little over a week, but it feels like ages since Jim has seen the outdoors. A little fresh air would be nice, even though it might be cold and rainy, our typical fall-into-winter Seattle weather.

Not wasting any time, Kim says, "OK, let's go!"

We're ready to walk! *Gulp.* This is a big step. I hold my breath and watch in amazement as Jim, assisted by Kim holding his gait belt, walks out of his room and down the hall.

You know those moments in life that take your breath away? Giving birth to a child, watching a sunrise from the top of a mountain, falling in love for the first time. That's exactly how it feels in the moment. I don't even have words. I just follow Jim and Kim down the hall to a physical therapy room.

Jim hasn't been out of bed in eight days. He's also anemic and still has to rehab his knee from the ACL surgery. It reminds me of an infant first learning to walk. I want to clap with each step he takes—I'm so proud.

Kim is extremely patient and kind, yet firm, urging Jim to keep moving forward. "You're doing great, Jim—keep going. I know you haven't been up and about in a while, so just go slow. I'm right here if you need me."

"You OK, honey?" I ask when they pause for Jim to catch his breath.

"Yeah, it feels good to be upright but I'm definitely winded."

Kim lets Jim stop as needed and keeps a firm grip on the belt. "Almost there!" she encourages him.

During our long, slow trek down the hallway, we run into an older gentleman who has a gentle, sweet face and very kind eyes. Kim introduces us. "Jim and Peg, this is Shawn. He's one of the volunteers here at the ARU."

"This is the first time Jim is up and walking," I explain to Shawn. I give him the short version of how Jim ended up in the hospital, then he shares his story.

"They didn't think I was going to walk," he tells us, with the clear triumph of someone who survived a crazy ordeal. "I was a quadriplegic after I had a spinal surgery, but I beat all the odds...and here I am. I enjoy hearing other people's stories and watching them make their own miraculous recoveries. It sounds like it's a miracle you are even alive, let alone up and walking after eight days. Keep up the good work, Jim."

"Shawn is our ARU cheerleader," Kim tells us as he walks away. "He's a volunteer and has really helped the therapists by showing our patients that anything is possible."

We keep walking, and Kim finally gets Jim to the physical therapy room. "Let's do some baseline tests to see where you are." She has Jim lie down on a mat and checks his knee's range of motion. I frown and quickly gather that Jim has suffered a setback with the knee rehabilitation. Kim reads the notes from Jim's last PT visit to see how much progress Jim has lost since he's been in the hospital.

"You've probably lost ten days of rehab on your knee, so instead of nine months to a full recovery, it might take you ten."

"At least I'm alive to rehab my knee," Jim quickly says. Admittedly, given what he's been through, an extra month doesn't seem so terrible. Next, Kim wants to test how far and fast Jim can walk. I am still so pleased that he *can* walk that I'm amazed she's asking for more. Kim tells Jim to rest on the mat in the PT room while she sets some things up. She returns shortly and announces, "Jim, we're going to see how far you can walk the ARU square in six minutes. You might make it half a loop, or maybe you can do two or three loops. We do this test when you first arrive in the ARU, and then an exit test to gauge your improvements and to see if you're ready to go home."

For the first time, Jim seems hesitant. "OK, I'm a little nervous about this," he admits. "This is a lot for my first day walking. I already feel tired and worried my legs might give out."

"I know it's a lot, but I guarantee that your body will recover the faster we get you stronger," Kim replies. "I set up chairs at the end of each hallway, so if you have to rest, sit down in the chair for as long as you need to. I won't stop the clock, but that's just fine. Ready? Let's go!" Kim says enthusiastically.

I watch in awe as Jim starts walking. It's a bit like he's drunk. He's still weak. He looks like he's probably lost ten pounds, and he's paler and gaunter than I've ever seen him. It looks like he just got over a bad flu. Because of the knee surgery, he keeps throwing his left leg out in a circle, not quite able to bend his knee. And of course, after lying in bed for eight days, he's super stiff.

Kim is well trained and carefully walks beside Jim, ready to grab his gait belt while giving him enough room to get his sea legs back. Again, I am overcome with emotion. Tears come to my eyes as I watch my husband, in a sense learning to walk all over again.

In his typical stubborn fashion, he pushes himself to do one complete loop before sitting in a chair. Jim even almost makes it a second loop before Kim commands him, "Stop."

He is more than grateful to sit down. He slumps into a chair as Kim checks his heart rate. "It's in the high 120s. Just sit there a minute and let it come back down."

Jim and I learned a deep breathing technique from a physical therapist who visited us on the eighth floor days ago. "Smell the roses, then blow out the birthday candles," she coached Jim. I remind him of this now, and his heart rate slowly lowers.

"That method works like a charm," I remark. "I am so proud of you, honey—that was amazing. Why don't you rest and when your parents show up, we'll surprise them by walking down the hall to the dining room?"

He laughs. "It'll be like them seeing their little boy taking his first steps all over again!"

After Jim catches his breath, Kim walks us back to his room to rest up for lunch.

When he settles into his bed, I take a moment to check in on his field. Wow, what a difference! Just the act of walking has changed my husband's energetic structure. There is something known as Earthing, a process where people walk barefoot on the Earth to give themselves a charge. I sense that Jim walking has reconnected his foot chakras and brought some much-needed Earth energy into his field. Overall, his field is brighter, the layers of his aura are in alignment, and he looks less pale.

My husband almost feels like himself again.

He falls asleep as I work. I don't wake him or move until I hear my phone ding. I had texted Logan earlier, asking him to let me know when he arrived with Carlos and Cookie so we could surprise them with Jim's walking progress.

I slowly stir my husband awake. "Honey, your parents are here. Should we walk to the dining room and surprise them?"

He takes a quick drink of water before we head out.

I put on the gait belt as I was instructed by Kim and start walking my husband down the hall. The look on Cookie's face is priceless. Full of complete and utter joy and astonishment, like we're witnessing a miracle. And in a way, we are. "Amazing, isn't it? He's like Superman!" I exclaim happily.

Cookie is actually rendered speechless, but Carlos is grinning ear to ear. "You look fabulous, son."

We all make it to the dining room so we can eat lunch with Logan, Carlos, and Cookie. Jim's appetite has improved, so Logan picked up sandwiches and chips. I am happy to see my son eating, but still note that he looks a little pale and gaunt—like Jim. His haggard appearance reminds me of the therapy appointment I booked.

"Logan, Maureen struck out finding a CISM therapist, but she did find one who specializes in trauma. I booked an appointment for you to go alone tomorrow, then I'll join you once Dad gets home," I say.

"Sounds good, Mom," he replies. "Honestly? I feel better already watching Dad walk down the hall."

I nod. "Still, I think you'll appreciate talking to her."

I'm glad my son is feeling better, but I know from my training that when you let the trauma pattern stick in your energy field, it's like a sweater collecting lint. The lint ball gets bigger and bigger. It's much easier to handle whatever comes your way immediately and then move on. I'm hoping that if Logan gets in to see a therapist while the details of November 2nd are still fresh, the trauma of his Dad's CPR event will fade quickly.

We eat lunch, and then Logan gets up to leave with Carlos and Cookie. Now that Jim has therapy three times a day and the room is so small, we are doing shorter visits. I feel relieved that Jim's parents are finally getting some rest.

I walk Jim back down the hall, and we relax for 20 minutes until Jennifer, the occupational therapist, shows up at 1 p.m. Her job is to make sure Jim can perform basic life tasks before he goes home. These tasks include showering; dressing/undressing himself; and simple chores like laundry, putting groceries away, and doing dishes. Like Kim, she has a bright, sunny disposition. I briefly explain to her all that Jim has gone through in these last eight days since his collapse.

"My dad is the battalion chief at the Kirkland Fire Department, so I understand what you went through very well," Jennifer says. "The battalion chief is called in for the most serious situations where CPR is going to be used. In any case, it looks like Jim is recovering quickly. The ARU will speed up his healing even more." She smiles at my husband. "Today, we're going to focus on personal hygiene, starting with brushing your teeth!"

Jennifer puts the gait belt on Jim as a precautionary measure, and says "OK, let's see how steady you are standing at the sink," and then stands close by and watches him brush his teeth. "That looks good," she says encouragingly. "Just stand close to the sink and lean in if you feel faint."

Apparently, Jim passes the tooth-brushing test, so now it's time for showering.

Jennifer leaves to get shower supplies. She brings soap, towels, and the bandages she needs to cover Jim's IV in his right arm. The doctors left it there as a "just in case" measure but had capped it off. Jennifer tapes Jim's arm and then looks hard at me. "Jim is going to shower on his own, which means you do not get to help him at all." I realize in that moment that I have literally been doing everything for Jim: helping him dress, making sure he takes his medications on time, and bringing him whatever he desires in the moment. Essentially, I have become so in tune with Jim that I am at his beck and call. Life is sending me a clear message. *Time to back off and let him figure it out.*

Jennifer walks Jim into the bathroom and locks the adjoining door, then guides Jim into the shower fully dressed. She says, "For the first few weeks you are home, I want you to sit down to shower so you don't fall and hurt yourself. You've already been through enough!"

Jennifer pulls up a chair outside the shower to make sure he doesn't fall. I am standing in the doorway and can hear Jim struggling to get his non-skid hospital socks off his feet. It takes all of me to not run into the shower and rip them off. I can see Jennifer eyeballing me, though, so I quickly back off. This is only Jim's second shower, and although it takes him five minutes to undress, he does pretty well with the rest of it. I can only imagine how awesome it feels.

Jennifer hands him a towel, and he dries himself off. She then has Jim sit in her chair to get his new socks on. It takes him almost 45 minutes to undress, shower, and re-dress. Jim is breathing hard and wiped out from the effort. Jennifer walks him back to the bed. "Jim, you did really great today. Rest up for ten minutes or so before your speech therapy, OK?"

"Gladly, and thank you, Jennifer."

I grab a warm blanket from the nurse to cover Jim and get him warm and relaxed before the next therapist shows up. I'm more than a little impressed. The ARU is the real deal—they push their patients hard! I hope this means that my husband will be home soon.

Promptly at 2 p.m., Megan arrives for Jim's speech therapy appointment. She is more serious and subdued than Jennifer or Kim, but this seems perfect for her more cerebral job.

"Hi Jim, I know you're probably tired from your big day. My name is Megan. You are going to sit in the chair and do some tests to gauge your problem solving and memory skills."

Jim is a little irritable and tired at this point. "Fine," he sighs.

Megan guides him from the bed to the chair and then puts Jim through a series of memory and mental tests. I can sense that he is getting overwhelmed, which leads to confusion. I sit on the bed watching Jim's responses as he works through these tests. They run the gamut from putting sentences into sequence, to remembering and repeating what you just read, to solving word problems and matching items. After 30 minutes of testing, Jim sticks his tongue out in a gesture of deep concentration. I stifle a giggle. He looks like a little kid trying to figure out a complicated math equation. I have seen my brother do this most of his life, but my husband? Never.

What was funny at first starts to trouble me. What does this mean? Has Jim's brain been affected when he died three times? He had done one short-term cognitive test before coming to the ARU, but that was it. I notice he is having a tough time focusing today, and his processing speed is slower. I feel panic arising. What if Jim can't hold down a job? And being the sharp and ambitious person he is, how will *he* feel if he loses some mental faculties? I take a moment to recite my mantra: "Love will get me through this if I remember to surrender, allow, breathe."

Megan does one more test, then smiles at Jim and says, "We're done for today! You did an amazing job, Jim. You should be very proud of yourself." She helps him back into bed to rest before dinner.

Jim and I both nap. He's exhausted from all his efforts, and I am emotionally wiped out from the thrill of watching him walk again. We are still drifting in and out of sleep when Alima comes by at 5 p.m.

I want to jump up to greet her but am too tired to get up. Alima glides in like an angel and is quickly at my side. She grabs my hand and gives it a squeeze.

Maybe she *is* an angel? She looks ethereal and a lot younger than her 70-plus years.

"Thank you so much for coming, Alima! You know it means the world to me," I say with the utmost sincerity.

"I can see you need more help than Jim at the moment," she replies, giving me the once-over.

"Thank you for coming, Alima! I agree that Peg needs help," Jim pipes up.

I smile. So glad Alima and Jim agree that I'm a helpless mess. Alima's always been one for candor. And while it used to bother me in the past, I'm just glad I now have someone to talk shop with.

"True. I don't feel good at all. I have all this stuck energy in my third chakra that makes me feel like I've lost my appetite. Most of the time, I feel like I'm going to throw up."

Jim and I hadn't talked in depth about my "crash" yesterday, but he could sense that I was suffering. And, even though he claims he isn't very intuitive, he knows that if I asked my teacher to come to the hospital to do an energy healing, I must really need it. Jim is content to lie on the bed and relax as Alima starts to work on me.

"I can see that you weren't kidding, Peg—your system is crashing." Alima is reading my field and assessing where to start work on me. Because she has worked on me before, she's intimately familiar with my energy patterns and usual flow. I am generally deeply connected and grounded, since I run Earth energy all day. I've done so much work that my field is usually balanced and clear, and my chakras are open and spinning. I can tell by the frown on her face that she is concerned by what she is seeing.

After a few minutes of taking it in, she says, "Let's just start at your feet and do a mini chelation." A chelation is another name for an Earth energy healing. Alima taught us the steps to follow, always starting at the feet and moving up the body while running energy as we go, charging chakras and the client's field. Then we end at the head, closing with a blessing to seal in the work we just did.

The reason Alima is at Evergreen is because she had her own health scare a few years back, driving herself to the ER while having a heart attack and getting a stent put in. She completely understands the situation Jim is in and what I have been going through. I sigh and allow the stress of the last several days to melt away...at least, as much as I possibly can. "That feels good," I murmur as she starts running energy up through my foot chakras. I've been pulling up Earth energy for days, but I've been using it to charge Jim, not as fuel for myself.

Alima heals like I do in that she grounds, establishes healer's aura, and then becomes an open conduit for energy to flow through. Since we speak the same "energy healing" language, she knows she doesn't have to sugarcoat the messages that are coming in from Spirit. After about five to ten minutes of charging my legs, she moves to my third chakra. "Peg, you can let go now," she says, softly but sternly.

I look at her, puzzled. "What do you mean?"

Still concentrating on my energy field, she replies, "You've tethered your whole family. Somehow, you created a split in your cords coming out from your third chakra. You formed a lasso around Jim when he started to die on the floor in your hallway, and then, because you are corded to your children as well, you brought their energy in to strengthen the lasso and tethered Jim to you and the kids. He's been using these cords to ground to the Earth and stay connected to you and your children even though he's been floating in and out of the spiritual realms."

I'm amazed by what I'm hearing, and not in a good way. "Wow, did I do that subconsciously when I saw his chakras shutting down when he was dying?"

"Yes, I believe so. What I see is that you have a deep desire for him to live, and your love for him is very strong. What you did by energetically tethering him to you is the equivalent of taking a bullet for someone. This saved his life."

I frown. "But doesn't someone have a *choice* to live or die? I didn't think I had that kind of power."

She shakes her head. "If you didn't tether him, he wouldn't have had the choice to live or die—he would have died for sure. You have to stay grounded to the Earth through your first chakra in order to stay alive, and you tethered him because you saw he wasn't connected. Jim was literally ascending out of his body," Alima explains.

It seems like Alima is telling me I did a good thing, but I'm still troubled. "Did I mess with his karma? Was he *supposed* to die?" I ask quietly. I glance at Jim and see his eyes are closed. I am having a hard time processing what Alima is saying, and I'm wondering how Jim will feel about it.

She shakes her head. "If Jim was ready to die, you would have gotten a huge subconscious NO from him, so you wouldn't have tethered him in the first place. The tether you created with your third chakra corded to Jim and acted like a lasso that held him and prevented him from leaving the Earth plane. It was one link in the chain. If Jim had tried to ascend out of his body as he died, he would have hit a big energy block in his fourth chakra because of all the clots filling his lungs. And if Jim tried to go back down and leave his body out of his third chakra, he would have gotten lost and then had to find his way out of the Earth plane. When people die, they must ascend out through their head, or their crown chakra; if not, souls become lost or stuck on the Earth plane. This is why we have ghosts, or souls that need help to move to the next place. You probably saw this fourth chakra block and knew that he would have problems ascending, so you held him at his third chakra."

I breathe a sigh of relief. So even if Jim had died, his whole path to moving out of this realm sounds like it would have been godawful, according to Alima. I glance over at my husband again, and tenderness floods my heart to think of him braving that kind of ordeal.

"So, where has he been energetically, then? Today was the first day he walked down the hall, so does that mean he's loosening the tether? Does he have the strength to fully come back?" I ask.

"Yes, Jim reconnected with the Earth plane today," Alima says. "I think that's actually why I am here, to help you untether yourself from Jim and your children and start your own healing. Peg, you completed your task—now you need to let Jim continue to heal his body and bring your energy back into yourself. I can see that you struggled a great deal through this process. You did an amazing job surrendering to the Divine plan and letting this be his journey on one hand...but on the other, you refused to let go at all. In fact, Jim would've had to fight like hell to die and leave you, because your hold on him was so strong. I can see that you never gave in to fear, and there is a deep warrior spirit within you. After all I've taught you, I am

209

impressed that you listened to Divine guidance, followed the directions laid down for you, and let love lead."

I breathe deep, lean back, and close my eyes briefly. I slowly let tears slip down my cheeks. These don't feel like my usual tears of the last eight days—they feel like a release. I am popping out the other side of this trial by fire.

I glance up at Alima. "I did it," I whisper.

She smiles, and all I see in her eyes is compassion and acceptance. "Yes, you did. You offered Jim a healing space that transcended his personality. Jim's soul communicated with your soul. If he was in the third dimension or able to use his brain, he would have tried to rationalize or talk you out of tethering him. Because of your deep love for him and the cords that were wrapping around him, he was able to make the choice to *live*."

Alima works to clear the split and reconfigure my cords. Energetic cords are like ropes that we form with people we are in relationship with. Until today, I didn't know you could tether people with your cords, because what I learned in school was that their sole purpose is to act as a conduit of energy flowing back and forth between two people. Although Alima considers what I did to be healthy cording, it has maxed my system out almost completely. When you are in a relationship with someone, you develop energetic cords that link you, chakra to chakra. Jim and I have been together for a long time, so the cords flowing between us are strong. This is why I could connect with him subconsciously when he was dying. We were communicating in a different energetic dimension when he was dying.

A dark cloud passes over my joy. If I had received the message that he didn't want me to interfere with his cords by tethering him, I would have had to step away. I would have *truly* had to surrender. I don't want to think about that now.

"I'm so tired," I whisper.

"I know, Peg. There is so much that led up to your making a choice to tether Jim when he collapsed. If you hadn't gone through the four years of my school, and then done years of healing work through your practice, I'm not sure you would have been able to tether Jim, pull in your kids, *and* do healing work 24/7 for the past week. You have probably done at least a thousand or more healings in your seven years of practice, and this created a baseline for you to make choices from. If you didn't do the repetitive drills I made you do way back when, I don't think you would have had the strength, or knowledge, to step outside of the box and save Jim's life. All of your efforts have led to the best possible outcome for you and your children."

I let myself take in her words for a moment before I respond. "Wow, that's *big*," I say. I shake my head. "I'm in awe of all that's happened. I remember feeling like I was upleveling the past couple of years, and my healing skills were improving, but I didn't think I'd be tested in this way. I just thought I'd have a larger capacity to heal more people. Why did I pull the kids in to tether Jim?"

Alima takes my hand in hers. "Jim was on the edge. So instead of just wrapping one cord around him, you wrapped five. It's almost like you were reminding him of five people who desperately want him to survive. Take another moment and pause, Peg. Let it sink in. You've been carrying the whole family for *days*."

I look at my teacher. I can literally feel Alima creating sacred space for me to heal. I visualize my third chakra cords going back to shaking hands with Jim, then each of my children. When you are in a healthy relationship, energy cords look like a mutual shaking of hands; that is, you give the same amount of energy you receive.

I can feel a big shift in my third chakra as these cords go back to their usual pattern. The feeling of an elephant sitting on my sternum has gone away. I can take in a deep breath again, and as I do, I relax. "That's better," Alima says. "Feeling good now?"

"Immensely!" I gush. She seals in her work, and I ask her, "Would you check in on Jim before you go?"

Alima moves to Jim's side and he stirs awake. "OK if I check on your energy field?" she asks.

"Sure thing," Jim replies. By now, he's too aware of her legendary reputation to say no.

Alima does a quick scan. "I've been working on you remotely since receiving Peg's permission. The DVT in your left leg is thinning out. And the right leg should be feeling normal again. I don't see any more copper wires."

I smile at the look of joy on Jim's face. I don't think he has quite understood until this moment just how much energy work many healers in my network have been doing on him.

"That's great news about the DVT, Alima! And you're right—the right leg is normal again, so no more zings. But what about my lungs? Are the clots clearing out?"

"Yes," Alima replies. "It's taken some doing, but they are starting to disperse. Go gentle on yourself, Jim."

Alima turns back to me, and I quickly say, "I'm going to need more work done, and I think you should also work on Logan. Would you be up for that?"

"You bet—just text me when you get out of here and are ready for a healing."

I give her a big hug and whisper in her ear, "Thank you for saving my family." I'm not exaggerating when I say that. In a sense, I feel that Jim is here today because of everything I learned from Alima. I smile to myself. The velvet hammer has definitely served me well.

Jim and I sit in silence for a while before I say, "Did you hear what Alima told me?"

"Some of it, but I don't really understand. Did she say you *tethered* me?"

"Yes, you owe me big." I smile.

"Thanks?" Jim says, half a question, half gratitude. I can tell Jim appreciates my efforts but doesn't have his strength back to try and have an in-depth conversation about the specifics at this time. It's something we'll have to table for later.

That, and it doesn't really feel there are words adequate for the moment. And no matter how detailed Alima's explanation and my understanding of what happened might be, I still feel like I'm standing in the middle of a giant mystery. I have so many questions, many of which I know will never be answered.

Jim and I smile at each other. "I'm glad you chose to live," I tell my husband quietly.

"I'm glad you gave me the option," he replies softly.

Twelve: Empowerment

Two things became abundantly clear to me yesterday:

1. I have to allow Jim to struggle to get his socks on.

2. I have done my job. Alima released me from duty when she told me to let go. Peg-Wife signing off.

Now it's time for Jim to continue his healing journey on his own with as little interference from me as possible.

The thought that if I hadn't gone home to check on Jim the morning of November 2nd, he would have died in bed, is one that has occurred to me repeatedly in the last several days. While I'd prefer to shelve it as a morbid, unhelpful thought, mulling it over now fills me with appreciation and awe rather than panic.

I look over at my sweet, sleeping husband and wonder what "dying" was like for him? We have been so focused on Jim's physical recovery and just taking things one minute, one hour, and one day at a time that we haven't talked about the emotional and spiritual aspects of his collapse. There is so much that went on between us in his last moments that it may take months to comprehend. In our relationship, I am the messy, emotional one who has her crap spread out all over the yard. Jim is more closed and stoic; he keeps everything tight to the chest, and he isn't quick to share. Given that we seem to inhabit different emotional planes, I wonder if we will ever discuss the extraordinary events of the last several days.

And if we did, how would I begin to wrap my head around it all? I wasn't even aware of my "tethering" him until Alima mentioned it. It's a principle that I'd never even thought about...but in the world of healing, you learn something new every day.

Day three of Jim's stay in the Acute Rehabilitation Unit starts abruptly when the morning nurse comes in a little after 7 a.m. and flips on the lights.

"Hi, my name is Jill. I was just reading your chart. You've been through a lot, haven't you, Jim?"

"Uh, yes," Jim says, still not quite awake.

I get him some water and move to his side. Jill is friendly and chatty, despite our grogginess. "Jim, you've surprised everyone by healing rather quickly. Just be forewarned that your ribs may take months to heal. When you get high impact CPR, as you did, it breaks your ribs. That's not like breaking a bone; it means there are tiny fissures in the rib bones. These will take a long time, probably six to eight months, to slowly knit back together. Because you had so many blood clots, those are still clearing out of your lungs—hence, the coughing. How are you feeling this morning?"

Jim is more awake now, and I can tell he is happy to have some clear information about what's going on inside of him. "My cough keeps me up at night. Is there some other medication I can take so I can sleep better? The Robitussin isn't cutting it. And the other thing I noticed this morning is that my feet are swelling. What do you think that means? Should I be worried?"

"I'll call the doctor about the cough. Can I take a look at your feet?" she asks.

Jim pulls his legs out of the covers and shows her his feet.

"Oh my God, yes, you are auto-diuresing," she says.

"What does that mean?" I ask.

Jill turns to me. "Don't worry, Peg, diuresis means your body is trying to balance its fluids. There is a rise in urine production by the kidneys to get any excess fluids out. I am going to mark an X on Jim's feet. I want you to check periodically to make sure there is still a pulse. We worry about circulation with this much swelling, and we don't want Jim to lose his feet. Let me go get some compression tights to help with the circulation in your lower legs."

Jesus, he just started walking again yesterday, and now he can lose his feet? I do reverse Reiki to pull the fluid out while Jill is gone and stop when she returns.

"OK Jim let's get these on you. I would wear them for a couple of days or until the swelling goes down, and you may have to skip wearing shoes."

Jill leaves and I go back to reverse Reiki. I have discovered throughout the years of my practice that it really helps relieve swelling and pain. I'm hoping Jim doesn't have to wear his "mantyhose" for too long.

I work for ten minutes and check the X's for a pulse. So far, so good. His feet still have a pulse. I pause to take a break and text Alima so she can double up on the reverse Reiki to help get the fluid out faster.

I smile when I see a text from her from the night before. "Jim's leg is getting better. I saw the copper thing- weird. Your cords are better, too."

I text her back: "Cords way better! Lots of swelling in his left foot. Think that shit is moving out."

Alima responds, "If you are up for it, do reverse Reiki to pull it out. I'm doing it, too. And relax your muscles!" I love that she's asking me to do what I was going to ask her for. Clearly, she's up to her Jedi mind tricks again.

I smile and text her back: "Yes, in a clench pattern. I'm trying to massage my legs and arms to release. You could bounce a quarter off me."

I know that my body is going to need a lot of care when we finally get released. I have been in fight or flight so long I'm wound up tight like a spring, ready to pounce or run. Luckily, I know several great body workers and craniosacral therapists, and my sister's husband is a chiropractor. I'm hoping they can undo the damage I have done to myself. My knees seem to be the worst, especially my right one. I have a throbbing pain that shoots up the outside of my right leg, and the kneecap cracks occasionally.

My body hurts but my cords *are* better. I can actually breathe more deeply and don't feel like I'm going to throw up when I eat. There was a big energy shift in me yesterday when Alima said, "Peg you can let go now." I hadn't realized how tightly I was hanging on to Jim. I understand now why I've been so depleted; I've been put emotionally, physically, and spiritually put through the ringer.

Ever since Alima told me I could let go of Jim; I've been feeling like a caged animal sitting in this hospital. If tethering Jim and giving him the choice to live or die was my test from the universe, I can be assured that I passed. He's alive and healing.

In my healing work there is a point where you can feel the energy shift and the client takes ownership and control of their healing journey. I felt this in Jim when Alima untethered him. I know from experience that deep and lasting healing occurs when the person wants it for themselves.

I asked Carlos and Logan to come up for Jim's therapy sessions today and after I explain the details of the day to them, I quickly kiss my husband goodbye. As I step outside, the cool, fresh air hits my face and I close my eyes. For the first time in a long time, it feels good to just be out of the hospital and to feel like I'm heading back to my life.

My first stop is to pick up Makenzie from my sister's. Unfortunately, she has spiked a fever and has a sore throat. I drive her home and get her into a hot Epsom salt bath, then I ponder what to do with her this weekend since I know I'll be at the hospital. Sigh. I want to be home so badly. I expected my kids to crash eventually but was hoping they would hold off until I got their dad home. Too late...it's starting. I see it as a natural response to the immense stress our whole family has been under. That and most likely the impact of using my kids' energy cords to tether their Dad.

I decide to call my friend Deborah, who's a chiropractor and someone I can trust to take care of Makenzie like I would. She's happy to hear from me. "How are you? I haven't wanted to intrude, but I've been getting updates from your sister. Is Jim healing?"

"Jim is much better and he's in rehab now, but I need a favor. Makenzie is sick. I don't want to infect Carlos and Cookie, and I can't be home to take care of her. Could you take her for the weekend? She's at home now and could be picked up here."

"Absolutely. I'll get her at five."

"Thank you! Just text me with updates or if she gets worse."

"No worries, I've got this," Deborah replies.

I thank her, hang up, and help my daughter into bed. "Quarantine yourself in your room. Grandma is here, so you don't want to get her sick. Deborah will be here around five to pick you up for the weekend."

I get a thumb's up and a wan smile. Makenzie has known Deborah since she was in diapers and trusts my decision. I turn off her light so she can rest, and then I head to my bathroom. I'm tired of fielding one crisis after another, but still, I'm proud of myself for asking for help.

I shower quickly, get dressed, and dry my hair. I pop in to check on Makenzie one more time, giving her a kiss on her forehead. "I love you, hon. Be sure to just ask Deborah for whatever you need and text me if you get worse. I'll figure something out." I close the door to her room. I head downstairs and update Cookie.

"I'm heading back to the hospital now. Makenzie is sick, so just let her rest. Deborah is coming to get her around five and will take her for the weekend and nurse her back to good health. I don't want you or Carlos to get sick. Madison will come home later from my sister's house, and Blake is taking care of Landon."

Cookie looks impressed by my capacity to keep everything in order. "Sounds good, Peg. Just let me know what I can do to help. Is Jim doing well with the rehab?"

"He's tired but he's making progress. They think he'll be back home pretty soon...but we also know it'll take a long time for him to heal, so we're taking it one day at a time."

I give her a big hug before heading back to the hospital to relieve Logan and Carlos. The short drive gives me some time to think and reconnect with my mind, body, and spirit. These days, I am getting more sleep, and I don't feel that bone-weary exhaustion and mental instability that I did when I crashed. My spirit is strong, and if anything, I feel a deeper connection with the Divine. I send out thank-you vibrations on the threads that connect all of us. Everyone's prayers, good thoughts, and acts of kindness have made a difference. Through all the highs and lows, and the terror of losing Jim, love has proven its magic.

I arrive back at Evergreen and find Jim, Logan, and Carlos in the physical therapy room with Kim. Jim is exhausted and needs help up off the floor and back to his room, where he immediately crawls into bed. Logan and Carlos take that as their cue, wave goodbye and leave, assuring us they'll be back soon.

I go into the hall to ask a nurse for a warm blanket and return to find Jim asleep. I cover him up and take a moment to sit and just gaze at him. He is looking less like a beat-up drug addict, and more like the man I married. His arms are still purple, but at least they stopped poking him to get blood. I get up and check the X's on his feet and find a strong pulse. I do reverse Reiki to suck more toxins out of his feet. Just walking has helped push the fluid out. I hold his feet and check in on his field. Now that Jim is "untethered," I can see all of his field layers. One, three, five, and seven act like fences, holding in layers two, four, and six. Each has vibrant colors, and there is no longer a block in his third layer and third chakra preventing Jim from coming all the way down into his lower chakras.

Energy flows up naturally through the foot chakras and down through the crown chakra at the top of the head. It can also flow side to side. Jim's energy system is starting to return to its natural state. I can still sense energy blocks around his ribs, lungs, and heart, which I know directly relate to the clots, broken ribs, and cardiac arrests. I'm glad that this part is pretty straightforward; what I see energetically relates directly to the physical problems Jim is experiencing. I sigh, realizing that these three areas of Jim's body are going to take a very long time to heal. I seal in my work and settle into the chair next to Jim.

I close my eyes and let my mind drift. I wake up to Jim looking at me.

"Hi babe, how are you feeling?" I ask aloud. "More of you seems to have come back today. Once you started walking it reconnected you to the Earth. And the swollen feet mean the toxins are clearing out. Your brain is sharp. I was worried the first day that you had some brain delays."

"I'm surprised, but it feels like I'm starting to trust my body again," Jim replies.

I smile to myself. It was only 24 hours ago that Alima was here. I'm still processing the fact that I tethered Jim, and what that means. There's still a nagging sense of not fully understanding what has happened. I am sure I will need more healing for me, Jim, and our children.

Jim has improved leaps and bounds after just two days of therapy. I am glad he hasn't suffered any setbacks from the rigorous schedule of three appointments a day. He is completely off the oxygen, and his nervous system is starting to calm down now that he is trusting his physical body again. Before he walked on his own the first day in the ARU, it felt like he was struggling emotionally and physically, but now he feels calm and centered. The more he walks on his own, the more grounded and connected to Earth energy he becomes.

I promised Jim I would stick by his side until he gets discharged, which means another dreaded night in the hospital. I settle into the cursed recliner, and try to sleep but find I am completely restless. Finally, I give up on sleep altogether, and sit quietly in my chair, breathing and trying to find a place of surrender - and allow the universe to provide. I feel raw—like someone took a cheese grater to my body, heart, and soul.

Jim starts to stir shortly before 7 a.m., opens his eyes, and looks at me. Day four in the ARU has commenced. "Good morning." His voice is starting to come back, and one of the speech therapists had expressed that whispering might actually cause more damage long term, so Jim has been trying to talk, but it sounds gravelly.

"Good morning, honey. How are you?"

"I'm tired, and ready to go home." I take a moment to check in on Jim's field. What I know from healing school is we are born clear of any energetic blockages and establish our own field layers at around six months of age, when we start individuating from our mothers.

At some point in our development, we start to experience the world, and inevitably, something happens to hurt us; abuse, injuries, bullying, traumatic events, and even shame and guilt can create an energetic wound. We start to defend against the wounds, rather than show up as our pure, whole selves, building layer after energetic layer to protect ourselves from getting hurt again.

What is interesting to me, is that even though Jim suffered a deep trauma, dying multiple times in the process, he is currently undefended, open, and soft, unlike his usual intense and anxious self. I can sense a deep shift in his field. It's like the trauma of dying didn't create a wound, but rather, broke his field apart and cleared some of the old wounds. My ability to do energy work to guide his fractured aura back together has helped him heal, and I am happy to witness him coming fully back into his aura now that he is walking, and his body is getting stronger. I marvel at the beautiful symbiotic relationship between the body and the energy field, which help each other function and flow properly.

Carlos walks into Jim's room a little while later, after being dropped off by my dad. I greet him and let him know I'm going home to shower.

"I'll be here with Jim. No rush," Carlos replies. I am guessing that the thought of losing his son terrified him so much that he's eager to be part of every step of Jim's healing journey, even the mundane parts. Whatever, the reason, I am grateful.

I head out to the car, excited to escape again and shower two days in a row—what a luxury! I love the cold, crisp feeling of fall. The world itself feels new and bright and shiny, like I'm rediscovering it; every little aspect of being back in it excites me: the smell of the air...the bustle of people going up and down an escalator...the Christmas decorations that just appeared in the gift shop. The past ten days have felt like ten years.

**

Day 5 in the ARU is a carbon copy of Day 4. PT, OT, Speech Therapy, lather, rinse, repeat. I have pulled back and keep taking Carlos up on his offer to be there for Jim's therapy sessions. Jim's brother Dave flew in last night, so we end Day 5 by watching the Patriots game.

Dave pulls a recliner into the common room so Jim can comfortably watch the game. It's the first television show we've watched in 11 days. It's almost like we're hanging out at home as a family, but we're in a hospital. We have taken over the entire common space. Jim seems to be one of the few patients who has a ton of family members visiting at all hours of the day.

This is all that matters: these people, this family, our love for one another—that's it. Every single second we live and breathe is a gift. I pull up a chair next to Jim and pull Landon onto my lap. "You're getting too big for this," I tell him, sighing in contentment. I swear he grew a foot and gained ten pounds in the past 11 days.

What should be a seemingly innocuous football game elevates Jim's heart rate and completely exhausts him. To say the least, it makes me question if he can go home tomorrow. *How are we going to make this work?* I wonder. We fought for Jim to go to the ARU because he was panicked about going home without oxygen and didn't feel he was strong enough. Now I am concerned that he's not as ready as he thinks he is.

I guess the hospital isn't concerned. Day 6 dawns when the morning nurse walks in and greets Jim and I a little after 7 a.m. "Hi Jim, what do you think...should we try and discharge you today?"

Jim's answer is resolute. "Yes! I want to go home."

I suck in my breath and put on a forced smile. I have to believe the doctors won't release him before he's well. Inside, I am doing a happy dance because I am ready to go home, but I realized last night that this hospital stay is just the beginning of Jim's recovery. Instead of having doctors, nurses, and therapists to help with Jim, now it will all fall on me.

"OK, let me get the ball rolling so we can get you out of here. I need to put in a request with Dr. Landover." (She is in charge of patients in the ARU.) The nurse turns and leaves without elaborating on how long this will take.

Makenzie is home sick today from school, which has me worried. Not for her, but for my husband. Jim has been through enough, and the last thing we need is for him to get a bad cold or the flu. After all his coughing in the past eleven days, I can't even entertain that thought. I'd like to keep him in a bubble until he has his strength back and his lungs are cleared. I am hoping that my energetic bubbles are sufficient.

The nurse comes back in our room and announces that he's made his request. "It's Dr. Landover's call now, so just wait to hear back from her. Until she comes to clear you, we'll continue with the therapies you have scheduled for today, just in case she wants you to stay longer."

Jim and I immediately look at each other. His face is determined and stony, and I can practically hear him saying, "There's no freaking way I'm staying in this hospital one more day." It reminds me of dating a horrible boyfriend or girlfriend; you put in the time, wait for things to change, and when you're done...you're done. Jim has done his due diligence and is ready to break up with Evergreen Hospital. Today is the day.

"Let me check in on your field, and see what's going on," I tell Jim.

I haven't done much energy work on him in the last couple days. After he started walking and we got most of the swelling out of his feet with reverse Reiki, I have purposely left his system alone. I always try to allow for integration time between sessions with clients. Often, just by nudging the energy system or raising the vibration of someone's field, you put them on the path of healing and need to allow for things to percolate. Jim has been through so much I want to give his system time to shift naturally.

I hold Jim's feet and instantly drop back into healer's aura. I am relieved I haven't lost my touch. I smile when I see how much healing Jim's energy system has done. He is no longer like Humpty Dumpty, and the "egg" around him is intact. The one thing I make a note of is that his chakras are spinning slower than normal, which I attribute to the heart stoppages from a couple weeks ago. I hold the seventh layer to give Jim a nice juice-up. Sometimes, getting an energy healing is like plugging yourself into a wall socket until you feel charged. I spend ten minutes with him, and satisfied that he has enough charge, I seal in my work.

"Yup, you're ready," I say. "But you definitely have a lot more healing to do. My guess is it'll take a full year or more for your system to come back online. However, I think it's safe to go home now and let you heal on your own schedule."

He heaves a sigh of relief. "I'm not exactly looking forward to the year ahead, but I'm grateful that I get to have it! Can you help me get my socks and shoes on? I guess I need to ready myself for one more day of therapy."

Jim's swelling from the auto-diuresing has gone way down, and of course I cave and help him put on his compression stockings (I'm a slow learner). What a joy to discover

his feet fit in his shoes again.

"Victory!" I exclaim. Jim has been wearing silly non-skid hospital socks for the last few days, unable to comfortably put his shoes on.

I take a moment to pack up all our belongings, even though we don't have an official confirmation of discharge. I can't get out of here fast enough. Then I realize I need to let our family know our plan. I text Dave right away: "Jim wants to come home today."

He responds: "I understand. Almost two weeks."

I reply: "Me too, I have chair ass."

At 10 a.m., when Jim's physical therapist Kim comes to get him, I find myself getting concerned that we haven't heard one word about Jim's discharge, nor have we seen Dr. Landover.

"It's good to see you, Kim," Jim says sincerely. "Two things: My shoes fit again, and I want to get out of here today!"

Kim smiles. "OK Jim, I'll make sure we re-test your strength and stamina and see if you pass so you can get cleared. "

She puts tape marks on the floor like she did the first day Jim got to the ARU. Then she asks Jim to get up from a chair and walk around the tape and back to the chair. I can only imagine the difference from Day 1 to 6.

Kim quickly confirms for me that it's significant. "Wow, you did that in 11 seconds, Jim! Just five days ago, you were at 19 seconds!"

"Good, did I pass?" he asks. I can't help but laugh. Jim is all about results.

"Yes. I realize this seems like a silly exercise, but at 19 seconds, you wouldn't be able to cross the street in time at a crosswalk; however, at 11 seconds, you would make it across."

What a grim thought. People might be strong enough to come back from a stroke or heart attack, but then they stand the danger of getting hit by a car if they don't walk fast enough. I have a whole new perspective on what it must be like for people with disabilities...things they must worry about that I have never even thought of until now. I feel silly for my outburst with Dr. Landover when I exclaimed I couldn't take Jim home on oxygen. I'm sure she has sent people home in worse shape.

"You ready to do some loops?" Kim asks.

"Now that my shoes fit again, and I don't need to wear a gait belt, yes!" Jim responds.

Jim is like a man possessed and takes off like a rocket. After two laps, he's tired but determined not to use his chair as a pit stop. His sheer enthusiasm heartens me.

"Keep going, honey!" I can hear the *Chariots of Fire* theme song in my head.

Jim doesn't rest even though he is breathing hard. He tells me later that he was motivated by the thought of using his own bathroom. I can't say I blame him; the last time I had to share a bathroom was back in college.

"Jim, you did three loops!" Kim says.

"Good, did I pass?" He can see the goal line—his own bed and pillow.

"You did! And if you leave today, it's been a pleasure working with you."

I give her a giant hug. "Thank you for your kindness and for helping Jim. There's no way we could have done this without you!" Indeed, the therapists in the ARU are saints in my book. I can only imagine what they have seen and helped people through.

Kim smiles. "He's a trooper. I know he's going to be fine."

We head back to Jim's room, and I take a moment to text Dave: "We are trying to get out of here. Director has to approve his release tonight."

No sooner do I finish texting Dave than I get a phone call from a number I recognize as Landon's school. My heart sinks as I step into the hall to answer it.

"Hi, this is the office calling from Three Cedars Waldorf School. Landon is in the health room with a high fever."

Worst news ever to receive as a parent, and the worst possible news to receive when Landon's sister is also ill and I'm trying to bring his not-fully-recovered, weakened father home.

I feel like crying but fall back on the second half of my mantra: *Surrender, allow, breathe.*

Nope, nothing...no surrendering, allowing, or breathing. It feels like I'm going to pass out from holding my breath. I turn to Jim's classic "smell the roses, blow out the birthday candles" trick. Success! I feel my system relax and calm down. I shake off defeat and jump into mommy mode.

"Oh no! Thank you for calling. My parents will come and pick him up."

After I hang up, I call my mom. I don't beat around the bush. "Hi, Landon's sick. Can you and Dad go back to school to get him, please?"

My mother says apologetically, "He looked a little funny this morning and was super tired. I'm so sorry, Peg! We should have kept him home or at least checked for a fever."

I grit my teeth, smile, and then respond, "Well, it's water under the bridge now. You can get him from the office." Then I hang up. I've never been good at saying goodbye to people over the phone, and my family constantly guilts me for hanging up abruptly. But today I'm frustrated, so I'm not feeling particularly guilty. All the same, I owe my mother so much for helping me these past two weeks, so I remind myself to make it up to her later.

Then I call our naturopath, Dr. Monster, whom my kids love. There's a 2 p.m. appointment that I take.

Next up, I call Dave. "Bad news. Landon is sick at school with a fever, so my parents are picking him up now and bringing him home. I need two things from you: Could you call the Marriott and book your parents a hotel room for the next two weeks? The last thing I want to do is get them sick." I continue "Also, I booked a 2 p.m. appointment for Landon with our naturopath. With Jim coming home, I can't take a risk that he has something serious, so I think it's better to get him looked at."

Dave teases, "Gee, Peg, what do you do for fun around here?"

"Nothing, apparently! I'll text you a photo of his health card and the naturopath's address. It's at least a half-hour ride from our house, so give yourself 45 minutes, just in case."

We have a saying in our house: "If you're not early, you're late." For me, punctuality is a way of witnessing and honoring others. Especially with what we are going through, even two seconds can make a difference. After all, what if the EMTs had shown up two seconds later?

Dave confirms that he's on it. I hang up just as Jennifer, the occupational therapist from the first day, shows up for Jim's appointment.

"Jim, would you like to fold laundry today or go on a field trip?"

The choice is obvious. "I think I'll choose the field trip."

"I heard you want to get released, so I'd like to take you for a tour of the outpatient rehabilitation and get your appointments lined up for you," Jennifer tells both of us.

She gets out the wheelchair while I go ask the nurse for a hot blanket. I love the idea of a field trip and feel like a first grader going to the zoo for the first time, even though we're just going outside to cross the street.

I follow as Jennifer wheels Jim out of his room and toward the elevator. I think she took the long way, but we both enjoy the walk and the fresh air once we hit the street. We emerge from the hospital into a beautiful sunny, clear-skied day. I turn my face to the sun. It almost feels like a coming-out party for Jim. *Ta-da, he's back!* I think to myself.

"All of your outpatient therapy appointments are in one building. You should continue with your physical therapy exercises daily and then have a therapy appointment twice a week."

"Not once a *day*?" Jim teases.

We arrive and are given a tour of the facility. It's about 20 times the size of the ARU therapy space and has at least ten therapists working on clients. We are introduced to the receptionist, who books Jim's appointments starting next week. Jennifer walks us back across the street, and we pause for a lunch break. Fifteen minutes later, the speech therapist, Brenda, shows up.

"Wow, you look fantastic compared to when I last saw you," she exclaims when she walks in. She had done Jim's initial cognitive test when he was still on the eighth floor.

Brenda and Jim get to work. I know Jim thinks these "mind riddles" are ridiculous, but by now he knows that he just needs to do an hour of testing to get cleared to go home.

After the speech therapist leaves, Dr. Landover finally shows up. "Jim, I heard you want to go home today. I have to tell you, we normally discharge our clients in the morning," she says hesitantly.

Jim's face clouds over. "You know, everyone has been great, but I feel like I'm ready. I'd like to go home *tonight*."

Clearly, this isn't Dr. Landover's first time at the rodeo, and I imagine she's faced many patients on the verge of tearing their hair out to get home. "I hear you, Jim. The problem is that the insurance companies sometimes won't pay the therapists if the client leaves the same day."

Jim doesn't bat an eyelash. "I will pay them myself."

I can see Dr. Landover soften. She can probably tell that arguing with Jim is futile. "Look, Jim, we can sort it out on our end. After reviewing the physical therapy tests and talking to the speech therapist, we all agree you can be discharged."

"Thank you for understanding, doctor. I know how much everyone has done for me, but it's time. Can I ask you some questions, though? I haven't heard a lot of the details about my case. Do you know exactly how many times I suffered cardiac arrest and how long each heart stoppage was?"

The 911 report has all the details, but it isn't something either of us has looked at yet.

Dr. Landover is clear and concise. "From reading your chart, I believe you had three cardiac arrests, with each requiring between five and ten minutes of CPR to bring you back."

I suck in my breath. I know he coded three times, but what she is saying is that he "died" for possibly 30 minutes. I wish Jim had seen the light or something other than just taking a dirt nap. As a healer, I am in touch with the Divine on a daily basis. I would have liked for Jim to experience the profound beauty and peace of the other side.

Then again, maybe if he had, he wouldn't have chosen to live.

"How do I not have brain damage, then?" he asks, incredulous.

"Because the paramedics performed what they call high-impact CPR, or continuous CPR. That means you never had a lack of blood flow to your brain. You have them to thank."

"So even though I wasn't responding, they just kept going? Ten minutes seems like a long time. At what point do they just give up and pronounce me dead?" I can sense Jim is astonished and searching for answers as to why he is alive. He has been so focused on just getting well that he hasn't had time to think about what it took for the paramedics and ER staff to bring him back. Now that he's about to go home, an understanding of the bigger picture is necessary for his peace of mind.

"Well, Jim, there isn't really a time limit. I've heard of them continuing for a long time, sometimes 20, even 30, minutes."

My pragmatic husband then asks the doctor a very important question. "Can my wife and I have sex?"

I immediately flash back to middle-school health class where we watched the film about how babies are made. My face flushes in embarrassment.

Good lord, really, honey? I have to admit it's a good question, but admittedly, it's the last concern on my mind.

I love that Dr. Landover doesn't break character; she just continues without blinking. "Sex is the equivalent of walking up two flights of stairs, so if your heart rate is staying below 120, then it shouldn't be a problem."

My head swirls to an image I would like to erase: Husband dies from having sex too soon after three cardiac arrests.

Jim smiles at me, victorious. I just shake my head. Nope, not happening.

"Last one, doc. Does Xarelto have any dietary restrictions? Like, can I drink alcohol?"

This is going from bad to worse. Jim sounds like all he wants to do is get drunk and have sex! I grimace.

"You can have alcohol, but the problem is that you increase your possibility of falling. A fall right now could set you back a month or more in your rehab."

Thankfully, Jim is done. "Thank you for answering my questions, and for the excellent care. I'm sure I'm not a normal case, and all of your staff have gone out of their way to be kind and compassionate."

She smiles warmly at both of us. "I'm happy that everything has turned out so well for you, Jim. You are definitely not our typical stroke or heart-attack patient. You'll resume a normal life once you're done rehabbing. Your nurse should have the final paperwork soon. I'll go sign off on your release."

I kiss my husband as soon as we're alone. "I am *so* happy."

He smiles at me. "I know, but right now I need to rest—this has been a long day."

I get Jim tucked in bed and settle into my chair for what, thank goodness, is going to be the last time.

Jim and I are hanging out waiting for our paperwork when, finally, the nurse walks in with a big grin and our discharge papers at 4 p.m. "Big day, Jim—you're going home!"

I immediately text Dave: "We are done. Please come pick us up!" I start gathering our belongings and realize we have a lot more stuff than I had realized. Jim got a big sign from his office with an orchid, and he also has a bunch of his personal belongings here: books, glasses, knee brace, slippers, extra sweatshirts and jackets, and hospital goodies (like a pee bottle and spirometer). Likewise, I have half my bedroom with me. I bug the nurse one last time. "Can I get a cart?"

"Let me get someone to cover me, and I'll help you guys out."

A volunteer arrives to help wheel Jim out. Hospital protocol. We are quite the caravan as the nurse leads us to a service elevator. As we walk out on the main level, I see Dave and Carlos walking in.

"We're free!" I exclaim happily. After a few minutes, we are all loaded in our car. The ride home is surreal. Jim hasn't been out in the world for 12 days, and as strange as it is for me to drive away from that hospital, I can only imagine how he feels.

We pull into our garage, and I feel tears welling up. Spiritually, I feel a deeper connection with Jim and our families, but I am also emotionally wrung out from the ups and downs of his recovery. Not to mention how much my body hurts. My joints ache, especially the nagging right knee, and my low back and ass throb from sitting in that godawful chair to sleep all those nights. My brain is foggy, which I attribute to sleep deprivation. I am a mess, and yet I can't remember feeling this alive and happy in a while.

Jim is moving slowly, and the short step up from the garage is daunting. He has enough bend in his knee to shimmy sideways and into the house. "I'm so tired, honey. Can I head right upstairs to bed?" he asks.

This is the part I've been dreading. How is he going to handle the stairs? Luckily, we have a landing halfway up, so we agree to put a chair up there; he can use it if he needs to rest. I ordered two pulse oximeters a couple of days ago to measure his heart rate and oxygen levels. Jim still has anxiety that his body could abruptly shut down on him again. It's unlikely, but if he wants a $10 device to have peace of mind, who am I to argue?

Jim makes it upstairs and immediately heads to his own private bathroom. We are moving at a snail's pace. I don't want to freak him out, but I'm also scared that he'll die on me again. There is no hospital nurse call button at home in case of an emergency. We have both been traumatized and it surfaces the instant we are home, so I'm just glad Maureen cleaned my rug and there are no reminders of that horrible day.

I get Jim in bed and ask what he would like for dinner.

"Who's cooking?" he asks.

"We have MealTrain food coming."

He frowns. "What's that?"

"Everyone wanted to do something to help us, so Stephani set up a Meal Train for us. All people have to do is log in and sign up to deliver a meal to our porch."

"Wow, people really *have* stepped up, haven't they?" Jim is incredulous. I realize he has been lying in a hospital bed and doesn't know about all that's been going on behind the scenes.

I tell him about Caring Bridge and how people across the country have been praying for his recovery. He just shakes his head. "I had no idea. I don't think I'm hungry, though. I just want to sleep."

"I'm going to take a quick shower and then I'll join you." I ask Jim's Dad to sit with him while I shower and change, realizing we are probably going to need a babysitter for my husband for the foreseeable future.

My post on Caring Bridge sums up my feelings about coming home:

> *I will not lie. I lay down in bed next to Jim and wept tears of joy, gratitude, and thanks that we've been given extra time as a couple and a family. Our story is so miraculous it doesn't feel like ours. Jim made the comment today that if you didn't know us, you*

would think we were making it up. It is so
fantastically outrageous! We love all of you for your
prayers, kind words, and concern.

Jim and I just lie in bed looking at each other, we smile. Although, he has lost weight, still has deep purple bruises on his arms, and has shrugged off death three times, his eyes are bright and I can feel his spirit: soft, palpable, and present. My husband is here with me.

We are both exhausted; we fought hard and we won. I'm reminded of all the tests and trials that we've weathered over the years: Logan's diagnosis of NF1, kid injuries and stitches, Jim's neck surgery, my tonsillectomy, the changes I experienced in those four years of healing school. The lesson in each of those moments, especially this one, is clear: Don't lose yourself. Stay grounded, ask questions, and most importantly, if you don't know the answers to all the questions that come up, find the people who do. And above all, keep the faith. Because it can mean the difference between life and death.

Thirteen: Healing Lessons

I feel like I just experienced another four-year healing school in twelve days—with much higher stakes. After getting a few nights of sleep and regaining some semblance of what it feels like to be human rather than a sleep-deprived zombie, reality sinks in that I had been irreparably changed by the last two weeks.

I know from the trauma patterns I have seen in my own clients who experienced life-threatening incidents like this one, that it is imperative to start our families' healing process as soon as possible. And the way I treat life altering experiences like this one, is that there are always lessons to learn along the way.

Healing Lesson #1 – Talk therapy combined with energy work is a powerful cocktail that speeds up the healing process.

Other than getting sick and being stressed, Madison, Makenzie and Landon seem like they are holding their own. Logan and I need the most help because we both witnessed Jim's collapse. Maureen found a great trauma therapist, Valerie, whose husband had his own close call with death. I leave Jim with his Dad and Logan and I head to our first appointment together.

As soon as I begin talking, I realize just how much PTSD I have from Jim's collapse. "I am literally sitting here completely antsy and ready to jump out of this chair," I tell Valerie. "Before we left the house, I stood frozen in the front hallway, wondering if I should come or not."

Valerie nods sympathetically. "This is all normal. If you hadn't gone back to the house the day of his collapse, Jim would have died. If you hadn't called 911, he would have died. You've stuck by him almost every minute of the last 15 days, so it's no wonder you feel the weight of this responsibility to be there at every waking moment. It reveals the depth of your love."

I sigh and feel myself relax instantly. "I didn't think you could just die like that. It was so disturbing. I don't think I'll ever get that image of Jim on the floor out of my head."

"You and Logan are experiencing classic PTSD symptoms, and neither one of you could ever be prepared for an emergency situation of that magnitude," Valerie said.

"I felt so bad leaving Logan in the house where his dad had just died on the floor." I look at my son and start to cry as memories of that day come rushing back.

Logan puts a hand on my arm. "Mom," he says gently, "I feel guilty you had to go to the hospital on your own. I'm OK, really."

After this first session together, Logan and I attend six more sessions with Valerie, together and separately, which helps us process the event and the aftermath. One point it drives home is the fact that if I hadn't turned my car around that morning, Logan would have found his dad dead in bed. I don't think I could have lived with myself if that had happened. I can finally see that I was divinely guided that morning and did right by my son.

Healing Lesson #2 – If you do energy work to heal the trauma pattern as soon as possible after the trauma occurs, it doesn't stick in your energy field.

I had asked Alima the day she untethered Jim and I in the hospital, if she would come to our house and do energy chelations for Logan and I, knowing we would both need energy work immediately.

Alima starts with Logan, and to support him I act as healer assist, holding his feet and helping him find ground again. His field looks like one of those snake-shaped fireworks—all curled up and grey with ash. I immediately feel my eyes fill with tears but remind myself to hold neutral for my son and allow Alima to work her magic.

Alima notices my reaction. "Peg, hold steady, we *will* get him unwound," she murmurs.

Logan looks back and forth at us, slightly alarmed. "Do I want to know what that means?"

"Just that when you were spinning in circles like the Tasmanian devil when Dad collapsed, you literally wound your energy field super tight," I explain, not wanting to freak him out but also feeling it is my duty to be explicit about what had happened in that moment.

"Great," Logan groans. He has allowed me to work on him over the years and put up no protest when I asked if he would be OK having Alima work on him. Given all he had been through in his life, he is very open to all kinds of alternative therapies.

With me holding his feet and grounding him to Earth, Alima is able to unwind his shoulders and open his field up again. Logan had sucked up his field to escape the trauma and was in a deep contraction.

"Feeling better, Logan?" she asks.

"Hmmm, yes, that felt strange." Logan doesn't quite understand what is going on with his field, but I can see the grey areas (which represent his fear) dissipating and his field getting brighter.

After a few minutes, Alima is satisfied with how his body looks and moves to his head.

"Yikes, I thought his body was wound tight," she exclaims. "His head and neck are *really* locked up."

I grit my teeth but continue to hold neutral and help my son ground. Alima holds his head and just follows his energy to assist his healing process. This allows Logan to heal himself, and we simply follow his lead on where the energy should go. The concept goes back to the idea that the body knows what it needs to heal itself. After about 15 minutes, Logan visibly relaxes and softens, and I can see the trauma pattern moving out of his field.

Healing Lesson #3 – The body knows what it needs to do to heal itself. Learn to listen to what that is.

Yoda strikes again, I think to myself, internally cheering. I almost wish I'd asked Alima to do this sooner but I was too absorbed at the hospital with Jim's recovery.

"Let me seal in my work and then we're done," Alima tells Logan.

"Feel better, son?" I gently inquire.

"Yeah, but now I need a nap. Thank you, Alima."
After we finish, Logan wanders off to take a nap, and
Alima stops to say hello to Jim on her way out.

"Jim, you look great! From what I can see from
having done some remote work, your DVT is almost
entirely gone, and you're doing the best thing possible for
your healing: resting quietly. Just give yourself time."

He smiled at her. "I will, Alima. I've made it clear I
can't have visitors for a while. It's all I can do to get up and
go to the bathroom!"

Before she heads out, I load Alima up with chili and
cornbread from the Meal Train deliveries so she will have
dinner for the night. "See you tomorrow for my session," I
say, giving her a giant hug.

The next morning Alima comes back to work on
me, and just like in the hospital she gives it to me straight:
"You thought Logan was wound tight, but you're still
pretty bad yourself."

"I know," I say, not in the mood to pretend. "I think
because I tethered Jim and looped my children in as well, I
was literally gripping the Earth for dear life. My legs feel
like I was hanging onto the edge of a cliff for a month, and
they've stiffened up from being stuck in one position too
long."

"Exactly! Let's see if we can unwind some of the pattern and get you relief."

It's hard when you're a healer to not help when you are getting work done on you, but in this case, I knew that Alima was happy for the extra help. I close my eyes and try relaxing my system. Just like the second night after Jim's event when I came home and tried to sleep, and the day I crashed, my body begins to jerk and shake.

"Should I be worried about this?" I ask Alima.

"No, let's just let your body shiver and shake until it clears the clench pattern."

Fifteen minutes later, I am actually able to lie on the table without twitching. I take a deep breath in and release it with a long exhalation.

"You are intuitively clearing yourself," she encourages, "so keep going with it."

A few more breaths and I feel a weight palpably lift from my body. A few pounds of stress...totally sloughs off. "I was in complete terror the first week in the hospital," I tell Alima. "Could you please check to see if I have a terror pattern in my field and clear it if so."

"I agree and find it remarkable that you were still able to work on Jim and tether him in spite of that. You intuitively knew what to do, even though your human side and ego were freaking out. Do you feel like the terror is falling away now?"

I check in with myself, do a body scan, and then answer, "This is going to take some time. It's almost like when you give birth. I feel lost and out of control, but I know in time I'll find my way again."

"Exactly, so be gentle with yourself." Alima charges my chakras, does some brain-balancing work (almost like flossing your teeth, but with your hands) on my head, and then seals in her work.

I slowly get up off the table and hug her. I almost feel like myself again. My brain fog has cleared out. "I really wouldn't be OK without your help. Thank you."

I see her out and go take a nap with Jim. "Feel better, honey?" he asks.

"Deep healing definitely occurred, but I have more work to do. I've addressed my immediate issues, though, so I just have to allow more of my healing to happen once we get you back on track."

Jim takes a long look at me. "I think it might take some time for all of us, but I'm glad we have the support we need. Especially you, Peg. You're so busy taking care of me that I sometimes worry you're not getting the help you need."

Healing Lesson #4- Self-care is one of the most important pieces of healing work.

I give him a kiss on the cheek. "I know, but it's going to be OK. And no more talking, please. After all, sleep is part of healing!"

Woven into healing Logan and myself is getting Jim to all of his doctor and therapy appointments. He is vigilant about his home physical therapy exercises and slowly begins walking a quarter-mile loop at the park just down the hill. He also has to graduate out of speech and occupational therapy, which includes getting cleared to drive again. During that process, on top of everything else, we discover Jim needs glasses.

When Jim collapsed, we were in the middle of a remodel on our home, so one of our first outings after his release from the hospital was to the local furniture store to pick out a couch. A short journey turned out to be somewhat labor-intensive, as Jim would walk, sit down, rest, walk, sit down, and rest in succession. The next day, we went to the bookstore and I had to ask a clerk for a chair so Jim could sit down before he collapsed. It was a struggle at first to gauge what Jim was capable of, given his stamina, which was slow going compared to his usual levels.

Carlos and Cookie stay until just after Thanksgiving and then fly home. Blake is able to work until mid-December, so that gives me the freedom to just be with Jim and focus on his continued recovery. My parents stay through Christmas and drive Landon to school every day.

Healing Lesson #5 – Don't overstep your boundaries, healing is a choice.

At the end of December, I finally get an appointment to see Loretta Brown, the other healer who worked on Jim and me remotely. Alima had taken care of my energy field, and Logan and I agreed that the therapy sessions had greatly helped with the PTSD, but one of my deepest internal struggles was wondering if I had messed with Jim's karmic journey. As a healer, this felt akin to a doctor committing malpractice. For close to two months, I haven't been able to shake the deep guilt that I've been carrying around.

Was Jim really supposed to be here? And if not, was *I* the one to blame?

Loretta greets me with a big hug as she ushers me into her office. "Wow, you and your husband have been through hell!" she exclaims.

Predictably, I begin to cry. Since she'd only heard about Jim's ordeal from my friend Julie, I tell her the entire story and then ask the question I've been afraid to ask: "Did I overstep my boundaries as a healer by tethering Jim?"

Loretta works directly with guides and ascended masters, so she pauses and cocks her head, almost like she was having a conversation with them and waiting for their response. I sit and watch her as she waits for an answer.

"OK, this is what they are telling me. No, you absolutely did not. This has been scripted for a long time. You and Jim have had a few lifetimes together and came back together specifically so you could do this for him. He was meant to live, and you did not keep him on the planet against his will."

I cry even harder. "Are you sure?"

"Yes, Peg, all is well. The one thing you should know, however, is that this is your last lifetime together. Your actions have brought your journey together as souls to a close. So, enjoy the extra years you now have left together and fill them with meaning."

Healing Lesson #6 – Have you ever met someone and felt like you knew them from somewhere? Soul families travel together and typically have contracts of how many lifetimes they will spend together.

On one hand, I am happy and relieved to hear that I didn't mess up Jim's karma, but on the other, I feel a stabbing sensation in my heart to hear that this is our last lifetime together. What she said made sense, though. In fact, when I think about it, I am surprised we found each other in this lifetime. I had just quit college, Jim had moved across the country—and somehow, in the midst of these gigantic transitions, we both ended up at the same bar the night we met. I never gave anyone my phone number for safety reasons, but I felt inclined to give it to Jim.

Loretta hands me a tissue and takes a moment for me to let it all sink in. "Call me anytime, Peg. This is some really deep stuff that you have gone through, and it might take a while to fully integrate. I'm always here if you need me."

After my intense healing session with Loretta I think of all the wisdom I have gained since I started my own healing journey in 2001. I learned that the Divine doesn't have a score card, and just because you do good deeds, that doesn't make you immune to illness and death. I also had to abandon my idealized image of what healing means. I know now that being "perfectly healed" is an illusion. Healing isn't about perfection. Life is complicated, and the Divine plan is full of twists and turns. Surrender is a huge aspect of healing, which contains lots of unseen elements.

Healing Lesson #7- Being "healed" looks different for everyone.

Like I promised my clients, I start my practice back up in January. Maybe it's too soon, but I feel like it's time to get back to what I love – healing people. My mind races with questions as I wait for my first client: Am I really ready? Can I hold neutral? What if my healing skills have disappeared? I call it the Wizard of Oz syndrome: That is, will someone pull back the curtain and see who I really am? Of course, ten minutes into my first session I am back in my zone, the healing work feels like riding a bike; I jump back on and start pedaling like I have never stopped.

It was decided by Jim's work that the Pulmonologist would have the final say on when Jim can return to work. We are shocked to learn during our follow-up visit with Dr. Young in December that this will be shorter than we originally thought. "Jim, I can't say that you should take until February for leave. I feel you can go back in January and ease into it. I have never seen a case as severe as yours, and a recovery as fast. It truly is a miracle." Dr Young then turns to me. "Peg, you were a rock. I'm still very impressed with how well you held it together."

Healing Lesson #8 – Energetic healing speeds up physical healing.

Dr. Young leaves the room and returns with Jim's CT scan, and once we see it, I realize it really is a miracle Jim is still here. "If you look here at your left lung, Jim, you can see it is almost completely blocked, and your right one looks like you have chickenpox. If Dr. Harwich hadn't done the full dose of TPA, I don't think we would be here right now in this office."

Jim and I glance back and forth at each other. We never seem to know what to say when we hear news like this. Appointment after appointment, the therapists and doctors express their awe at Jim's story and recovery. And while I know that Jim received the best medical care possible, I have rapidly come to the conclusion that the energy work I did on Jim has only accelerated his healing time and results.

So, by January, Jim and I resume our normal routines: work, eat, sleep, repeat. With each passing day, I find myself breathing easier and easier. All of that ends at 4 a.m. on Mother's Day morning when Jim wakes me up with urgency in his voice: "Peg, everything just went black...it was like I died for a minute or two and came back online!"

"What?" I am bleary-eyed and confused, but my heart is racing when I hear those words.

He pulls his long-forgotten pulse oximeter out of the drawer. His heart rate is elevated and his face pale with fear.

"Should we go to the ER?" I ask, immediately bolting out of bed and pulling some clothes on, ready to act fast.

"No, let me see if I can get my heart rate down with some deep breathing."

I am now wide awake and terrified. After a few minutes, Jim's heart rate actually comes down, but he is cold and trembling.

"Honey, maybe we should go get you checked out," I repeat, my throat dry as I imagine many worst-case scenarios.

My stubborn husband is back. "No, I'll go see my regular doctor and get checked out." Which he did a week later...and he found nothing amiss. For my peace of mind, I check in on his field, which feels like it has undergone a reboot. Just his system working out the kinks. One of my psychic clients confirms my intuitive hit and tells me she thinks it is a brain reboot, too.

We go back to life as usual, although what we have learned over the past six months of being home, is our lives will forever be changed by this event.

Healing Lesson #9 – You hold emotional pain in your body which can become physical pain.

Over the next few months, I do some acupuncture, massage, bodywork, and craniosacral work to resolve the aches and pains that still nag at me. My right side took the worst of it. I am healing in fits and starts but still don't feel like myself.

Finally, in September, ten months after tethering Jim, I experience a breakthrough in my own healing. Once a month me and three other colleagues I now call friends: Kelly, Rachel, and Elizabeth, meet and do group healing sessions. Years ago, I taught them energy work, which led us to working on people in groups, until one day we had an epiphany that we should do these group sessions for ourselves.

We get together monthly and do round robins; this time, I am first on the table. My right leg still isn't 100% after my 12 days of sleeping in a chair and standing on the cement floor of the hospital for hours at a time.

Kelly takes her time and gently unwinds my right leg and I feel something release deep inside my hip. The phrase, "Your issues are in your tissues," definitely apply in this case. I have an instantaneous emotional response when the hip lets go, and start heaving great sobs.

"Peg, let it go…you have been holding all of this in your body, and that's why the pain hasn't disappeared." My time has ended, so I roll off the side of the table and stand up, drying my tears.

I nod. "I know that, but it's always hardest to heal yourself and realize to what degree you still *haven't* healed."

Kelly could see I still wasn't steady on my feet and came over to help me keep my balance. "Peg don't worry about the time. Try something for me. Can you walk backwards around the table?"

"Seriously?" I had never tried this method but could see Kelly was serious. I did three loops, and then something shifted deep within. I feel like I am walking back into myself. The best way I can describe it is, imagine you are hiking and spill the contents of a backpack all over the trail. I feel like I am going back over the mountain and collecting the belongings I lost along the way. Back into the Peg I left behind when I tethered Jim. I feel like I have been lost and have just found myself again. It is such a relief.

Kelly encourages me to keep walking until I finally sit down on the table and just let go. Alima had told me months ago to let go of Jim, but today felt like I finally *did*. These three beautiful women hold me and surrender to the moment. They are able to hold sacred space for my healing, and just love me for me. I have come through this crazy test because of love like this.

Healing Lesson #10 – Surrender to the "what is" and allow love to heal.

This healing session marked a dramatic shift in my healing. That feeling of being rubbed raw with a cheese grater dissipates and I almost feel like myself again. I still question tethering Jim and if that was the right thing to do. When this crosses my consciousness, I go back to my conversation with Alima. She told me in the hospital, "If he didn't want you to tether him, you would have heard NO in your subconscious and not done it." I believe Alima, trust what she said, and definitely feel like I passed a challenge of sorts...but did I, really? Is Jim supposed to be alive or did I choose *for* him? That question may never be definitively answered but what I know is I won't be tethering anyone soon. It's taken me months to heal from it. On the flip side, would I change any part of this small piece of our lifetimes spent together? No. I love my husband and got him back, which does feel like it has all been written in the cosmos.

Epilogue

It's almost exactly one year after my husband died in my front entryway. Jim and I have both spent this past year healing in our own ways. Jim sought answers in the form of details, whereas I looked for the deeper spiritual meaning. After we returned home from the hospital, Jim, true to his analytical form, requested we go to the local firehouse and obtain the 911 report that gave us details of his CPR event and a list of the firefighters and paramedics who came to our aid. We also requested his medical records from Evergreen Hospital. This led to hosting a gratitude party in April with family, friends, and anyone involved in Jim's care, including nurses, doctors, therapists, firefighters, and paramedics.

After meeting at this party, we forged a friendship with one of the paramedics, Chris Ingebritson. This in turn led to Jim and I volunteering to be a part of the Medic One Gala by filming a reenactment video of Jim's story. We discovered that Medic One is a program unique to King County, Washington. According to their website, the Medic One Foundation "is privately funded and raises money to support paramedic training and continuing education, targeted research, and medical oversight of paramedic performance. The Foundation has set the standard for pre-hospital emergency care in the U.S." In short, if you are going to have a medical emergency, Washington State is your place. The save rates are off the charts compared to other parts of the country.

After reading the details of the 911 report and the hospital records, it became quite clear to Jim and I that his chances of survival were slim to none, and because of where we live, we received the best paramedic response in the country. Thank you, angels!

Given all he went through, and how long he was clinically "dead," we are still shocked that Jim has fully recovered with no lasting side effects.

The changes within both of us are subtle yet profound. We don't necessarily spend a lot of time mulling over the miracle or even talking about it, and for our children, except Logan (who was there), Jim's hospitalization was just a blip on their radar. We are trying to take time to slow down, remember to call our aging parents more often, eat family dinners almost daily, and spend quality time with each of our children.

A few days after the gala, I startle awake when Jim starts poking me at 6:15 a.m.

I groan. "Glad you're still here to poke me awake." I lean in and kiss him. Today is Jim's "first birthday" after being reborn a year ago.

"Anytime," he says, a mischievous twinkle in his eye. He looks like himself again: big smile, laugh lines and all. Any traces of a major health crisis a year ago are gone, minus a slight limp at times.

I shower, dress, and get Landon ready. Madison is away at college now, and Makenzie is in France on exchange. Logan just got a full-time position at Costco and seems to have no lasting effects from the trauma we witnessed a year ago.

Although every single one of us feels battered and bruised in ways that are not always apparent, we have made it a year. It's a big day for Jim, but for me, it feels like it's time to close the book on this. No pun intended.

I kiss Jim goodbye one more time on my way out the door. I pause and look down at our hallway rug. It's about the only thing that is the same since Jim's collapse. At first, I debated about keeping it but now I see it as a badge of honor. The rug served a purpose in this event; otherwise, Jim would have been lying on the hardwood floor.

I tease Jim jokingly, "No more crazy antics like dying in our front hallway today, OK?"

"I don't plan on it," Jim replies.

Acknowledgements

There are so many people I want to thank: First, there's Alima Hamilton. You changed my life with your healing school, impacted so many others, *and* saved my family. Thank you for showing up in the hospital to heal me, and for your continued mystical wisdom. You are truly Yoda!

Sara Heisler, my sister and number one fan, kept cheering me on and telling me, "Yes, you can!" I am so grateful for her support throughout the entire process of being there for Jim, and writing my story in the aftermath.

To all of my husband Jim's family members, as well as mine—thank you for continuing to show up, support us, and love us through an event that changed our lives.

Mike Goehring, you're my hero. You always protected your little sister and jumped in to help without hesitation. I am still moved to tears by your love and kindness during my darkest hours and that this event led us back into one another's lives.

Myron and Wendy Thomas, you are rock stars! Without your love and support during this event, and in our day to day lives, I am not sure Jim and I would be doing as well as we are. You two know how much we love you. Thanks for being there every step of the way.

Maureen Wrast, only a true friend would clean my husband's blood out of my rug. You are a soul sister.

I also want to thank my dear friend Kelly McNelis; in writing her own book and sharing her own story, she made all things seem possible in sharing mine.

Thank you to my fearless editor, Nirmala Nataraj, you encouraged me to just start writing and helped shape this story.

Erik and Stephani Torgerson, we are so grateful for the incessant arranging of meals, ride shares, and tech support.

To the two doctors who made the tough call in the ER—and you showed me the delicate balance between life and death that brave souls like you have to deal with every day. Thanks for your knowledge and your courage!

I am so grateful for the three paramedics who issued life-saving measures—Jim Whitney, LaFond Davis, and Chris Ingebrigtson. You have taught us so much about the Medic One Foundation and their excellent training. You're like family to us now, because without you, there would be no happily ever after.

Made in the USA
Coppell, TX
12 March 2020

16781261R00164